JUN 1 1

THE L life

THE L life

EXTRAORDINARY LESBIANS MAKING A DIFFERENCE

ERIN McHUGH

PHOTOGRAPHS BY
JENNIFER MAY

STEWART, TABORI & CHANG · NEW YORK

For anyone who has ever stood behind a closed door
and wondered how they would find their way out,
this book is dedicated to you.

Published in 2011 by Stewart, Tabori & Chang
An imprint of ABRAMS

Library of Congress Cataloging-in-Publication Data

McHugh, Erin, 1952- The L life : extraordinary lesbians making
a difference / Erin McHugh; photographs by Jennifer May.
p. cm.
ISBN 978-1-58479-833-0 (alk. paper)
1. Lesbians—Biography. 2. Lesbians—Interviews.
3. Homosexuality. I. Title.

HQ75.3.M385 2010
306.76'63092273—dc22
[B]
2010005290

EDITOR: JENNIFER LEVESQUE
DESIGNER: CHALKLEY CALDERWOOD
PRODUCTION MANAGER: TINA CAMERON

The text of this book was composed in Whitman and Fresco

Printed and bound in Hong Kong, China

10 9 8 7 6 5 4 3 2 1

Stewart, Tabori & Chang books are available at special discounts
when purchased in quantity for premiums and promotions
as well as fundraising or educational use. Special editions can
also be created to specification. For details, contact
specialsales@abramsbooks.com or the address below.

THE ART OF BOOKS SINCE 1949
115 West 18th Street
New York, NY 10011
www.abramsbooks.com

Contents

Introduction

had no idea what I was in for.

Don't get me wrong, I knew what I wanted *The L Life* to be: a gorgeous, colorful, honest tribute to all kinds of lesbians who had made a difference—a difference in history, whether it be LGBT (lesbian, gay, bisexual, and transgender) history or otherwise; a difference to the world we live in. I wanted to focus on women who make a difference in the lives of people whose paths they cross. And I thought it would be easy to spot them, simple to pick them out of the crowd. But when we say, "We are everywhere," we're not kidding, though some of us are more visible than

others. In a world where there is still a glass ceiling for women, and with no Equal Rights Amendment, lesbians have become the secret love child of the invisible sex. In fact, throughout this volume, you'll repeatedly see lesbians identifying themselves first as women, or as feminists, before they label themselves as lesbians.

There are lesbians in these pages who are no strangers: actor Jane Lynch, movie producer Christine Vachon, comic Kate Clinton, sisters Amy and Elizabeth Ziff from the alternative rock band BETTY. These are women the lesbian community has long known and admired. And of course there are many who are not as well known—women we may have forgotten, or those who have not yet been discovered—who are silently making change every day. Each story is not only a snapshot of now, but a tale of how every one of these women became the heroine she is.

In *The L Life*, you'll meet a sheriff, a bestselling author-cum-cartoonist, a congresswoman, a social worker, a rabbi, a farmer, a doctor (and yes, there's a joke in there somewhere, though I'm not sure what it is), and many other remarkable lesbians. And of course there are the activists, women who spend their lives moving our agenda forward, one step at a time, sometimes in increments so tiny we can't see them until we look behind us. What they all have in common is something I find equally fascinating in art as well as in life: They are all wonderful examples of the bravery of ordinary people. They seem to live almost instinctually, acting according to what their hearts tell them—they are certainly not held back by public opinion. Many spoke to me of dinnertime in their homes as kids, with nightly discussions of politics, news items, or simply learning what's right and what's wrong. To all those moms and dads? It took.

And these women bestowed lovely things on me—show tickets, T-shirts, invitations to dinner, conversation in small-town gay bars, a ride in a police car (unmarked, no siren), books I might enjoy, a jar of honey, and a plate of poached eggs. Best of all, and most generous of all, they gave me names of the women they admired, people they thought I might just like to talk to, or lesbians they knew should be included in the book. Calls were made, introductions were offered, e-mails flew.

The L Life turned into a sisterhood. In an age where time is one of our most important commodities, it turns out everyone wanted to stop for a moment and think how they could help this cause, and this book, and complete the circle the women in these pages form. It felt old-fashioned, in the best sort of way, the kind of neighborliness history tells you America was built on.

These lives are triumphant, every one of them, though I think almost every woman here would tell you, "It's not over yet!" There are difficult stories of coming out here, of political victories, of fights . . . always the fight. I fell a little bit in love with every single one of these women, and I wish I had the words to thank them properly. I simply have never had so much fun in my life. I want fiercely to do them justice, and help them to share their stories. We would be extremely lucky to find a little bit of all of them in each one of us.

During the writing of this book, my wonderful photographer, Jennifer May, and I crisscrossed America to meet these women who would become new friends. During this incredible journey, I got to do some great American things that I've been longing to do for many years—see Dealey Plaza and gaze out that window in the Texas School Book Depository, ferry over to Alcatraz, and visit the United States Holocaust Memorial Museum in Washington, D.C. A film I saw there featured one of the rescuers a woman whose family had helped hide Jews from the Nazis. She reminded me of the preciousness of freedom and the terrors of discrimination in all its guises. "My mother said, 'If it's the last thing you do, you must prevent injustice,'" the woman on the screen remembers. She pauses, and then, almost to herself, says, "I don't want to live in a world where nobody gives a damn."

You won't find that here in these pages. Not once.

—ERIN McHUGH, NEW YORK CITY
August 2010

Kate Clinton

It's almost like being a lesbian is both Kate Clinton's vocation and her avocation. She takes it very seriously. It is not a hobby. It's not something she just does on the weekends. Kate Clinton is truly committed to bringing her people together, and getting them some respect and maybe even some equality. Perhaps she learned it all in her hometown of Buffalo, New York: "The City of Good Neighbors" (well, technically she's from Hamburg, which may be the first funny thing about her). "The weather is so bad," theorizes Kate, "that you *have* to be good neighbors."

In Kate's case, the good neighbor stuff began at home. The middle child of five kids, she found early on that the best way to both curry favor and protect herself was by making her siblings laugh. "We said the rosary after dinner, during which time my goal would be to get one of my brothers laughing. That was my early comedy training." But that was already Act II. "In first grade, I lip-synched 'I'm Getting Nuttin' for Christmas.' The audience was mostly made up of nuns, except in the fourth row was Miss Como—*mee-oow!* gorgeous!—who laughed so hard she nearly fell off her chair.

I thought, 'I like this!'"

A star was born.

Also present—or perhaps omnipresent—in Clinton's upbringing was the Catholic Church. She jokes about having made enormous progress as a "recovering Catholic," but it does seem that her sense of community, and of sharing, giving, and volunteering—which she does constantly, and with grace and aplomb—comes from what she calls the "good aspects of Catholicism." Of this she said, "When I was growing up, at least in *my* family, those aspects included that you visit the sick, help out at church, you donate—basically it was very much about service to the community. It was not about hating gay people."

By the time she was a teenager, Kate was beginning to suspect that she wasn't like the other kids. "I remember saying to my dad that I *really* like my girl friends. And he said, 'Well, we all really like our friends,' and I'd say, 'No, I really like my girl friends.' But he wouldn't pick up on it. In high school, I dated, but began to think that it was really going to be a lonely life, that I would end up darning socks." Kate lived at home while attending Le Moyne College, and looking back, says, "I haven't any real clear memories of college, because I was trying so hard not to come out."

Eventually she broke through and came out with a vengeance, of course, but admits even today, "When I get impatient with people for not coming out, I have to stop and remember how long it took me." But

Kate still had one career in front of her before she hit the stage, coming out night after night—a job that provided years of simulated practice. She learned to be quick on her feet, listen to her audience, and hone her style—all by teaching high school.

"When I first began performing, there were moments when I'd think: 'I will not leave this stage in a panic; I've been through this before,'" confesses Clinton. "'This is like the first day of school; you will be all right'. I definitely think it helped my delivery, and I plan a show the way I plan a lesson. My performances are all about having a lesson plan. It's great that people think that I am spontaneous and speak off the cuff, but I really love language and work very hard to get it right."

From English teacher (and girls' track coach) to the stage still took some doing. It sort of started on a dare, back in 1981. "I had talked with my friends about wanting to do stand-up comedy and one of them booked me and said, 'You're on!' We should all have friends that take us that seriously."

From the basement of the local Unitarian church, she could only go up, and before long she started to become the darling of lesbians everywhere. A combination of talent and heart is hard to beat: Kate Clinton, from the beginning, has shown up. Volunteerism, like activism, is part and parcel of who she is. From the LGBT Center in New York, where she seems in constant service as an emcee, to the National Center for Lesbian Rights in San Francisco, where she serves on the advisory board, to countless other events from coast to coast, Clinton offers up what people need, whether it's her sharp judgment, her fast mouth, or both.

Nothing is sacred on Clinton's stage: On American politics, she is smarter and wickeder than most comics. Women, feminism, lesbians, and the Catholic Church are all key ingredients for her comedic stew. She has said that the brain is a very sexy organ, and she uses it full force, on- and offstage.

Clinton's views on humor and the difference between men and women doing stand-up is also incisive and insightful. "If we allowed women to really be the kind of comics that men could recognize—men don't recognize it unless it's set-up/punch-line penile

humor—women would really be more circular and take time to develop something and maybe not get there. I think that is the kind of humor I most enjoy. Men say that women aren't funny, but that's because we aren't performing in a format they recognize."

Whether in their hometowns of Manhattan or Provincetown, Kate has a one-woman review board in longtime girlfriend Urvashi Vaid, who Kate says consistently says, "too long" after each performance. The audience never seems to agree.

So what about the future of Kate Clinton's comic journey? "I feel that I'd like to go a bit more universal," she muses. "I'd like to do more about the environment, aging, the economy, and I'd like to follow the discussion

Comedy: A Holy Moment

 In terms of performance, Catholicism has given me tons of material. I feel that I treat a performance as if it were a really holy moment, because there were times when going to mass worked for me. It is about community and people being together. Certainly there is the ritual aspect and there is the pleasure of seeing people week after week and all of that. For me it is like doing a show in a town and going back year after year and seeing people gather together again. So that kind of appreciation of Catholicism I have, but I always felt like an outsider. My brothers got to be altar boys; I got to clean up the altar. They tried to learn Latin, whereas I could recite the whole mass in Latin. I was always angry that there was no place for women."

we're having about race." We can also count on her to continue with her primary message, which she feels it is her lifework to spread: "Gay is good." And because a good deal of Clinton's job is not only to entertain, but to also incite and inform, her personal mission is "To smash the patriarchy," adding, more seriously, "and making sure that everyone has enough to eat."

She calls herself a humorist ("Because I hope they last longer than comics"), but other than that, Clinton defies labeling. "I think of myself as a woman, but actually, I do think of myself as a lesbian first. I reached this point by having my head jarred by feminism. I never felt I got the faith and religion from the Catholic Church that I believe my mother got. I was very jealous of her. When feminism came along, I felt like that was the religion for me."

Yet, like it or not, other titles do define her. She's an author and a performer, and she has been in films. And perhaps in the way Diana Spencer was the "People's Princess," Kate Clinton is the "Lesbian's Lesbian." Women seem to either want to be her, sleep with her, or both. Asked for a self-description, she at last relents and zings back, "I'm a happy medium."

Above all, Kate Clinton is one of our community's comic ambassadors. She's there to remind us of what's important, and what needs to be changed, but at the end of the day, she points out what's so funny about it all.

Alison Bechdel

Past generations grew up with the hijinks and escapades of Moe, Larry, and Curly; but once the 1980s arrived, there was a new crowd in town that appealed to young women coming up and out. *Hellllloooo* Mo, Clarice, and Sydney!

They were the brainchildren of cartoonist Alison Bechdel, born circa 1983 as the *Dykes to Watch Out For*. This gang was a group of friends living in a medium-size American city who spent nearly twenty five years growing up (if not growing too much older), breaking up, working, playing, having a few kids and lots of sex, raging, politicizing, talking, and teaching along the way, through everything from the AIDS crisis to gay marriage. Perhaps it's no mistake that the dykes often spoke out for women over the years when we seemed to be fairly quiet: from the end of feminism as we used to know it, right through to *The L Word* years. They were there for us to turn to for an entire generation.

If you take a close look at Mo, the queenpin of the dykes, she bears a striking resemblance to her creator.

She's shy, vehement about her beliefs, politically savvy, and wicked smart—a mirror image of Bechdel. But the cartoonist insists she's more than Mo. "They are each a little part of me," she muses. "I created these characters to be the fantasy community I never had." Bechdel describes the strip perfectly: It's "half op-ed column and half endlessly serialized Victorian novel." It's also totally hilarious.

Before we all met the dykes, Alison Bechdel went to college at Oberlin, and then worked at some temp jobs in New York, allowing her time to really work on her burgeoning talent. That career began with single-panel cartoon for *Womannews* newspaper in 1983. She soon realized that working in one panel was too limiting: There were stories to tell, and she simply needed more space.

So she turned *Dykes* into a full-blown strip. Soon there was the odd fan letter, and then a few other papers asked to run this hot new lesbian comic. Bechdel and the dykes temporarily settled in St. Paul, Minnesota, before eventually relocating to Vermont. At *DTWOF*'s high point, sixty to seventy newspapers ran the adventures of Mo and her posse. "I started making $15 a strip. Sadly," she said with a laugh, "it never really went up much from there." The dykes are now in retirement—a very difficult decision to come to, the cartoonist admits—while their creator continues her pursuit of another cartoon form altogether . . . because Alison Bechdel caught a current in the mainstream that she never saw coming.

"Confessional" and "cartoonist" are not two words

that generally go hand in hand. But neither are the phrases "graphic memoir" and "*Time* magazine Book of the Year." Yet, in 2006, they came together for the first time in publishing history. It was then that Bechdel wrote *Fun Home*, the story of young Alison's quirky family, her realization that she was gay, and, ultimately, the shock in finding that her troubled, intellectual father was also homosexual. By the time she was in college, Bechdel's father was dead—of an apparent suicide.

Fun Home is poignant, honest, loving, and funny. It succeeds because it has both a linguistic and visual point of view; it is much, much more than the sum of its parts. How someone takes on their family, warts and all, and shares them with the world seems like an extremely brave effort. But the author disagrees. "My mother would say it's indiscreet," she admits. "I had to do it. I didn't feel like I had any great amount to lose, so I don't know if that counts as bravery. I felt a catharsis, but maybe not in the way I thought I would. It was mostly that I was just able to remove this huge amount of data from the hard drive of my brain."

What is fascinating is that when Alison Bechdel goes to speaking engagements and does readings, she finds that *Fun Home* has reached an audience far beyond what she ever could have imagined. About half the crowd, she marvels, are straight kids reading her book for a class; there are also mothers who are reading it for their book clubs. She insists that she did not see this success on the horizon, and comments on it

with her characteristic modesty: "It seemed like a crazy story to me! I was in the right place at the right time for both those tracks—graphic narrative had been gradually evolving toward mainstream acceptance for some time, and so had gay narrative." But she believes what gives *Fun Home* its universality is that "it's vicarious . . . people love seeing someone else tell the truth about their family secrets—because everyone has them."

True enough. But there is another constant is her writing. From dykey friends struggling to find their place in a largely straight world, to family searching for happiness in each other and themselves, one thing is clear, though the author herself may disagree: Alison Bechdel writes love stories. And we're all invited to share in the love.

Separate and Unequal

 The most difficult part of being a lesbian was when I first came out *and* realized I was going to be out and be a professional lesbian. I felt like I had gone beyond the pale, like I was not a part of polite society, and it was difficult. It enabled me to thrive and do my own work, but it also made me cloistered in that way. But it was painful, I felt like it was separate and unequal. I didn't really feel like I was good enough. *But* . . . it's also the feeling that fueled my work in *Dykes to Watch Out For*. I was so determined to show—at least to myself—that lesbians were humans and that their stories were worthy human stories that deserved to be read by everyone. I was able to prove that to myself ultimately. But it took a lot of doing."

Marjorie Hill

Marjorie Hill is nearly impossible to miss. She has been on the forefront of LGBT activism in New York City, and a staple at fundraisers, award ceremonies, and events of all kinds. She can be found anywhere the community gathers. If you've managed to miss her name in the newspaper, or on a committee list, it's pretty hard to miss Marjorie in person: She is a six-foot-tall African-American woman—until recently, with long, long dreadlocks—as statuesque as a queen, impeccably turned out, often with an African-print shawl slung over one shoulder.

She is definitely a presence. And now that presence is felt every day somewhere almost no one saw coming: as CEO of the Gay Men's Health Crisis (GMHC)—the world's oldest HIV/AIDS service organization.

Even as a child, Hill was a star and was filled with the kind of idealism she would later need to take on the kind of career whose mission it is to tackle a pandemic. As a little girl, Marjorie was put in an intellectually gifted children's program, and she was the only African-American in the class, with the additional burden of being trundled across the city during the earliest days of busing. The story of Hill's very first day, traveling from Bedford-Stuyvesant in Brooklyn to Ridgewood in Queens, is heartbreaking in its innocence. "My mother was a little concerned about sending her seven- or eight-year-old on a bus. I came home after my first day at school very excited and I said, 'Oh, Mom, it was great! We got there and they had a parade just for us with signs and everything. They were making noise and it was just great!' My mother said, 'That's very good . . . and they may have a parade again tomorrow.' They were demonstrators. It wasn't until the following year when I was a little bit more sophisticated and there were no clowns and no music, just angry white people, that I realized what was going on."

This was perhaps Marjorie Hill's first lesson about being different. "It was a weird kind of experience being an outsider in my class, being an outsider on my school bus, and being an outsider in my neighborhood." Looking back now, she realizes, "The thing that I hadn't thought about but did occur to me later was that those early years were an opportunity for me to prepare for being a lesbian."

Coming out was a gradual process for Marjorie, as it is for so many. She recalls first getting her hackles up when her then-boyfriend jumped on the Anita Bryant bandwagon and opined, "Gay people shouldn't teach." "I was incensed," she recalls. "I don't think I was even in touch with why I was so angry. We had a really huge argument and I said something like, 'I can't believe you're that stupid.' He said to me, 'Well you'd better be careful defending gay people before somebody thinks *you're* gay.' And I said, 'So what?'"

A summer job during college brought the inevitable summer love. "I had boasted to all of my friends that when my mother was ready to know, I would tell her." But when the time came, and her mother got curious, Marjorie balked at first. "I felt bad, but I couldn't tell her. About two days later, I arrived home about midnight and woke my mother up and told her that I was a lesbian. She couldn't quite get what I was saying, but finally she said, 'What? What? You're gay? Well I'm happy; go to bed.' So I said, 'Mom, I'm a homosexual.' That, she understood. So she sat up looking very distressed and said, 'Are you going to quit school?' And I thought, 'Oh, God, my poor mother. She's having a nervous breakdown.' I told her that I had no intention of quitting school and she sighed and said, 'OK, go to sleep.' That weekend was fine, and on Monday morning as I was leaving to go to school, she said, 'Oh, have a good day—and tell that girl she can't come to my house anymore.' I respected that; it was her house. It was probably a year before I had anyone that I was dating over."

Hill continued her education until she received her doctorate in psychology. "I had a private practice in Brooklyn, seeing families, gay men and lesbians, and some children. I taught and did some clinical work, which I loved. My fantasy was that I would move to Atlanta, teach at Spellman College, have a private practice, and be a southern belle."

I Make My Choices as a Whole Person

 When I get up in the morning and have to walk my dog and brush my teeth, I don't think 'Power to the Black People,' or 'Where's my Rainbow Flag?' or 'Oh, yes, I'm going to write a check to Planned Parenthood in response to that horrible murder.' I'm thinking, I have to brush my teeth, walk my dog, and get my ass to work. When my partner and I are at Bloomingdale's and there are six white men being waited on, there is plenty of staff, and we can't find somebody to wait on us, I don't have the luxury of thinking, 'Hmmm, maybe it is because I'm black; maybe it's because we're two lesbians; or maybe it is because they only know how to help men.' I don't have the luxury of dividing myself into separate parts, nor do I want to. I am a complex individual who is really wonderful because I am an African-American lesbian woman. That's what makes me wonderful."

Then David Dinkins became the first African-American mayor of New York City, and Marjorie Hill's profession changed forever. Suddenly, the LGBT community had a real place at the table in New York City. "It was phenomenal," Hill recalls. As far as Dinkins was concerned, "this was not just an idea, but a principle. When he talked about New York City being a great mosaic, he really believed it. The lavender tile was there."

"My title was liaison to the LGBT community. I'm not sure exactly what I expected, and I'm not sure that the administration knew what it expected. I did a lot of events, some with the mayor, some representing the mayor, and some just out in the community. We really promoted *Heather Has Two Mommies* and the Children of the Rainbow curriculum, having condoms available in public schools, and the syringe program began under Mayor Dinkins."

From there, Hill moved on to commissioner of the State Workers' Compensations Board, and then assistant commissioner of the HIV/AIDS Bureau at the New York Department of Health and Mental Hygiene. And her association with GMHC began in

1994, when Marjorie had joined the board of directors. A decade later, she became the director of the Women's Institute there, and then, took on her present job as CEO.

If you consider that the small band of men who came together to form GMHC and address this new "health crisis" in 1982 were well-to-do white men, like Roger McFarlane, Larry Kramer, and Edmund White, it is interesting to learn that GMHC's clientele was extremely diverse. "I think because so many white gay men were able to get their social service needs met elsewhere, our constituency was primarily less affluent white men, men of color, and women," Hill points out. "Today we see one third African-American, one third Latino, and one third white. And 25 percent of our clients are women. The women that we see are overwhelmingly African-American. Approximately 45 percent of our clients are over fifty, and we have a very strong youth program."

So if you still think it's unusual to have Marjorie Hill leading the charge nearly three decades later, listen up. "I like to provoke the truth. This is the job that I have been preparing for all of my life," she says with feeling. "It requires the right amount of clinical knowledge; the right amount of public-policy advocacy; the right amount of handling of donors, board members, and celebrities; the right amount of cheerleading for new staff; and it requires being able to envision a world without AIDS, while living in a world that includes it."

And if that's not clear enough, when asked if she considers running the Gay Men's Health Crisis a job about AIDS or a job about health care, Marjorie Hill's answer is swift, firm, and heartfelt: "It is a job," she says, "about social justice."

Jane Lynch

At the age of forty-nine, Jane Lynch became the lesbian "it" girl.

Oh, it wasn't like she hadn't been on the horizon for a while. In fact, she'd pretty much been on everybody's radar since she girled up with Jennifer Coolidge as the dog handler in Christopher Guest's achingly funny *Best in Show*. But then came *Glee*, and Jane, as Sue Sylvester, became the gym teacher everybody loved to hate.

When you meet Jane Lynch, she throws her arms open wide as if you're the ship that just pulled in to her desert island. She is over six feet tall, and the big laugh and easy grin of hers that one sees on-screen is clearly not just the work of an actor. That grin has been around: For many years she's been a familiar character actor with a surprisingly lengthy (and sort of nutty) roster of small-screen television roles, including *JAG*, *Gilmore Girls*, *Two and a Half Men*, *Frasier*, *Desperate Housewives*, *Dharma and Greg*, *Party of Five*, and, of course, *The L Word*. That's just for starters.

But it was Kellogg's Frosted Flakes that originally helped her turn the corner. Writer and director Christopher Guest has spent a good bit of his career directing commercials ("Whenever you see one that makes you laugh, that's his," Lynch

insists), and some months after he had directed her over a bowl of cereal, they ran into each other again. "I forgot about you," said Guest, and next thing you know, she was cast in his film *Best in Show*. It wasn't about getting on the fame map—for Jane it was being involved with what Guest was doing with comedy. "I remember seeing *Waiting for Guffman* and going, 'Oh, my God, I have to do this, I *have* to do this. *How do I get to do this*?' I don't know how I got so lucky."

But that's a long way from Port of Call, where Jane got the acting bug as a kid. "My mom and dad did shows. We had this thing called Port of Call in the school, where every classroom would have a 'port of call'—a Scottish room, an Irish room, an island room, and so forth. The shows would go on all night; you would do ten shows a night and the audience would go from room to room. I would go every night with my parents, and watch these forty-year-old women just living out their dreams of being a performer. It was singing and dancing and I was literally beside myself, having an out-of-body moment, thinking, 'I must do this.'"

Lynch kept this burning desire a bit of a secret, almost like the sexual orientation she was beginning to question. But her mother, who herself was partial to singing songs from *Man of La Mancha* along with the Saturday cleaning, discouraged her. On advice from Ron Howard and Warren Weber (Potsie from *Happy Days*), who were on a radio call-in show in Jane's hometown of Chicago, she set off to the Screen Actors Guild offices to procure names of agents. "My mother was rolling her eyes, and when I got home I started to write letters. She sat down and said, 'Listen, I know you want to be an actress, but there is very little possibility that you are going to do it. You can't be on TV if you live in Chicago.' She basically told me not everybody gets to do what they want to do. And I burst into tears. She thought she was helping me and she kind of crushed a child's dream." Well, not quite.

It didn't stop Jane from trying out for parts in high school. "I was almost too shy: I wasn't a shy kid, but I was afraid to ask to be in a play for fear they wouldn't let me and I wanted it so much. A lot of my childhood was stepping aside—I was just so afraid. In fact, the first play I got in high school, I quit. It was as if I walked into my destiny and it was almost too much. And I walked away from it."

So Jane went off to college—not even originally as a theater major—and later earned a scholarship to get her MFA at Cornell. "I loved it. It's theater boot camp. It's not an intellectual pursuit. You're not writing papers. You're fencing, and dancing, and doing vocal work, and working all day long and doing rehearsals at night or a play and going to bed and of course partying and getting up at six in the morning and starting all over smelling of vodka. . . . The theater!" (By now Jane's mother had come around to the acting thing: "If I could buy you a town, I'd buy you Ithaca," she said.)

Then came a short, unhappy stint in New York.

Jane Lynch, the Character

 I am fascinated with people who
wear their entitlement—or
whatever their psychological thing
is—on the outside and don't even
try to cover it. I'm always mon-
itoring—I'm a nice Midwestern
person, I'm always polite!—so I
love people who don't bother with
that stuff. I don't think I ever play
a person who's in the middle of
the road. They always have a little
something where you say, 'That
is *off*.' That turns me on, that
makes me laugh—because that's
the last thing I want someone
to think of me."

Lynch worked a nine-to-five job at a PR firm, drank too much, and moved seven times in nine months—the last time she just dragged all her stuff on the subway. She was not able to get any auditions. "I was dying inside." It was the same for a while when she relocated back to Chicago. She sent out résumé after résumé, until she got a call from the famed Second City—and suddenly she was touring with them and learning the art of improv. It gave her the skills and confidence she needed to try Hollywood.

Still, Jane was feeling anxious about her long-realized—and now unearthed—homosexuality. What troubled her most was that she hadn't told her family. "I started seeing a shrink, but I was really moving away from my family—they didn't know me anymore, and they could feel me pulling away. My therapist told me to write a letter, saying I never had to send it. So I did. I was really happy with it—as happy as one can be with a coming-out letter. Of course you're always going to send it: It frees you psychologically."

Within a few days, she'd heard from her entire family. "My dad said to my mother, 'What's the letter about?' And my mom said, 'Jane's gay.' He said, 'Is that bad?' And she said, 'No, it's not bad.' They all called me and said 'It doesn't matter. We love you.'"

Getting through her private storm seemed to open Lynch up to be what makes her so special to the LGBT community: She is not afraid to be an out lesbian in a business that makes it very hard. ("I hope that by the end of our lives being homosexual is about as important as being left-handed," she says.) Christy Cummings in *Best in Show*, a role she landed back in 1999, was her first star turn. It was the moment audiences said, "Oh, I know her. She's great." Then she took on *The L Word* as lawyer Joyce Wischnia. And though Sue Sylvester is written as a straight character on the show *Glee*, she is, after all, a pretty butch gym teacher.

Remember that Jane Lynch was never dragged out of the closet; she is absolutely guileless. When asked if she thought audiences were going to pigeonhole her as gay after *Best in Show*, she squealed, "No! I thought people were going to say I'm a successful actress. Look, I've been in a Christopher Guest movie—look at me!"

This all begs the question: From whence the normalcy? "I thought it was going to be a monumental thing, and how I felt about myself would change with some fame, but the thing is, because it's happening to me at forty-nine, at the end of the day I know who I am and nothing on the outside is going to change how I feel about myself, whether it's criticism or adoration. And I think I have much more equanimity about it than I would have had twenty years ago. And I love it, I think it's great, I love the affirmation, and for someone who's in comedy, there's nothing more satisfying than someone saying, 'You make me laugh so much.'"

Well, if this is what Jane Lynch's dream is, she's bound to be satisfied for a long, long time.

Amy & Elizabeth Ziff

Where *did* these two come from?

They poke at each other like kids, and protect each other like mothers. But ultimately, they are the personification of sisters. There is a bond between them you can almost touch—a stranger would not be wise to make a chance remark against one to the other. During Elizabeth's battle with breast cancer in 2009, she spent months at her sister's home, slowly recovering on the couch, with Amy's dog, Molly (the youngest Ziff girl), staunchly by her side.

If Amy and Elizabeth Ziff look familiar, then you're probably a BETTY fan. And if you don't know BETTY, you should: They are the longtime, quintessential girl trio (sometimes with a drummer and extra guitarist backup) that defies music industry description. Part rock, part a cappella, totally alternative, BETTY's Ziff sisters have also been the darlings of the lesbian community for more than two decades, with straight partner Alyson Palmer, a long, lanky African-American beauty, as their third.

Probably the best way to do justice to Elizabeth and Amy Ziff—and BETTY—is to toss a couple of queries into the pot and stir. (Or more likely, stir it up.) Get ready to be a a fly-on-the-wall and listen in. . . .

ELIZABETH: "She'll negate everything I say, FYI."

AMY: "That's not true."

Uh-oh, here we go. They are at once volatile and charming. One wonders if this sister act has been going on since birth.

AMY: "Our dad was in the military, so we lived all over the place. It was really weird because we were Jewish, and we never lived anyplace Jewish, so we were always outsiders looking in."

ELIZABETH: "We had to teach kids about Hanukkah and stuff in school. Which didn't go over well in Fairfax, Virginia. So that's where I learned to beat the crap out of people."

AMY: "I didn't beat anybody up. I killed them with laughter."

Oddly, characters from the novels of James Fenimore Cooper come to mind. One woman light, one dark—in both coloring and demeanor. It's not a good vs. evil pairing, exactly, but certainly two sides of the same coin. Tossed into the great wilderness of a new land, they each had to learn how to fight their own battles.

ELIZABETH: "Amy killed them with laughter, and I beat the crap out of them. It was tough being a Jew in a non-Jew place, but it taught me to be strong. My brother wasn't the biggest guy, so I had to protect him. I also beat up a guy in high school because he called Amy a kike. And they called my parents, and my mom said 'Good for her.'"

AMY: "As kids we hung out together; as teenagers we didn't."

ELIZABETH: "We were maniacs!"

AMY: "Well I wasn't. She was a rebel and I was a straight-A student. President of my junior and senior class, got in early acceptance at William and Mary—I was the consummate student."

ELIZABETH: "I lived in the smoking lounge, barely graduated from high school, and only because my English teacher was a lez and loved me, she gave me a D. And this was before I knew I was a lez. We never were mean to each other or anything like that—we just didn't hang out together. We were in majorly different crowds. I stole her car when I was fourteen. Made a key, stole the car, went out every day with my friends. Fourteen! Went down to the DMV with her birth certificate, got my picture on her license."

AMY: "Which I'm going to have to do now because I can't pass my driver's license test."

ELIZABETH: "Oh! You should definitely do that. You should! Why haven't we thought about that? Anyway, we drive back into school, me and my friends—we're smoking pot and eating McDonald's—we've been doing this for weeks, weeks!"

AMY: "And my gas was always lower, and I was always freaked out . . ."

ELIZABETH: "So I pull into the school parking lot, and there's the school principal, the police, Amy, everybody. So I just say '*Run!*' and we take off. I'm sitting in English, and there's a *knock, knock, knock* . . . I got majorly suspended for that. I got in trouble a lot. A lot a lot a lot. I still do."

The Ziffs had always played music, often together, as teenagers. But Amy, who is two years older, had other plans in mind for the future.

ELIZABETH: "We had a couple of bands before BETTY."

AMY: "I was in graduate school as a fellow at George Washington, teaching French, and I made all my students come to our shows. Then we met Alyson (BETTY's bass player Alyson Palmer) at a bar. We were in an all-girl band with her."

ELIZABETH: "Named Quiver."

AMY: "And on the side, the three of us would sing a cappella songs, make up fun stuff in the car. We surprised Dodie Bowers, the owner of the 9:30 Club in Washington, at her birthday party. It was our first performance as BETTY."

Now, if you've ever heard these three onstage together, you know that when they do their a cappella thing, it's about one step away from heaven. But it's more than just their angelic voices that make BETTY.

ELIZABETH: "When we all hit a note together, we still feel it, too, and it really affects people. That's why we're still together. That, and politics. And I think we don't do it just sonically, I think we do it viscerally. We do it with comedy and pathos and humor. . . . We're all individually activists in different ways, and together as BETTY we're activists. Our music isn't super political."

AMY: "We're all committed to doing things—to changing the world, really. Or changing a piece of it."

ELIZABETH: "We always have been. It's just been a part of who we were."

AMY: "We played in the very first gay pride parades, like Washington in 1987."

ELIZABETH: "Nobody would play them."

AMY: "Nobody would go there."

ELIZABETH: "And we played them: (a) because we wanted to go, and (b) because we wanted free drinks.

It wasn't our core crowd, but it became our core crowd. We had a kid's show on HBO; we've done a lot of stuff. Gay people take us as theirs, interracial people take us as theirs—I think that's great. . . . When we started doing AIDS work it was before AIDS had a name—it was gay cancer—and our friends were all dying. We started doing benefits and people said, 'You know, that's not really good for you. People are going to perceive you as being gay.' It was very different."

Ultimately, it's led to a long, successful career, with no end in sight. BETTY could stick a pin in more cities on a world map that they've played in than a USO tour. And it's been more than two decades of incredible, unforgettable moments, some of which the Ziff sisters are about to reveal.

AMY: "One of the best concerts was V-Day (a global movement founded by *The Vagina Monologues* playwright Eve Ensler to stop violence against women and girls) at Madison Square Garden—that felt very important to me. Not just because of the impact of the show and the concert, but it was a whole movement. And it was really exciting."

ELIZABETH: "The Ms. Foundation when we played with Pearl Jam and a couple of other people. There's been a million. A zillion. Australia was pretty fun. We had pot brownies and performed naked onstage. It was pretty great."

AMY: "When we played with Sweet Honey in the Rock."

ELIZABETH: "I think when we sang for Alyson's mom

when she was in the nursing home was our best concert. There are moments like that. It's not about the millions of people."

But sometimes it is in the millions. There is their involvement with *The L Word*, of course: Ziff fingerprints are all over it. From the theme song they wrote and performed, to Amy's appearance playing herself in several episodes, to Elizabeth's many creative contributions (yes, she's the "ezgirl" in the credits): co-executive producer, writer, and composer. And yes, Amy and Elizabeth even appeared as BETTY.

ELIZABETH: "It was an incredible opportunity. I think for us to have done the song, too, was important historically. A lot of people don't understand that. It was historical for the show."

AMY: "It's not just that it was the first time 'fuck' was used in a theme song. It was pretty strong; it was pretty feminist."

ELIZABETH: "It's a strong theme for a strong show. So that was great. Because one of my favorite things in the world is making CDs for people, and sharing music with them—for me to be able to turn literally millions of people on to music I like and love, and have them respond so intensely to it, and give people who would never be heard—really seen and heard—an opportunity to be featured on television? That was really thrilling and exciting."

What advice do they have for young girls coming up? They are, for example, absolutely gaga for Alyson's young daughter, Ruby, and protective as hell. The Ziffs care enormously about girls on their way to womanhood, and how the world treats them.

AMY: "Find an aunt, or an uncle—someone who maybe you don't relate to completely, but who you gravitate toward. Because I think that's a problem with traditional families—you don't see yourself in that. It's really hard to blossom."

ELIZABETH: "Move to New York, know your history."

To Wed, or Not to Wed

 ELIZABETH: "I do have a problem with marriage in general, because I think it's gross that in order to get certain legally binding rights, you need to be married. I believe in the complete separation of church and state. I don't think straight people should get married, I don't think gay people should get married."

AMY: "I'm into marriage."

ELIZABETH: "Well, dating isn't a problem for musicians, just FYI."

AMY: "I don't know if you should move to New York anymore."

ELIZABETH: "Move to a place with artists. Why do you negate everything I say?"

AMY: "Because . . ."

ELIZABETH: "Just say that for *you*, maybe, and *I* would like to do this."

AMY: "Well, I would say . . ."

ELIZABETH: "Just check off every time she negates me. It always starts with, 'Well, no . . .'"

AMY: "I wouldn't say move to New York. Before I would have said move to New York."

ELIZABETH: "Well, that's fine. I just think in terms of being a woman. You just need to be a feminist. What we've discovered is that you don't need to be a feminist to be a lesbian. At all. If everybody's not equal in the world—one people cannot be oppressed in the world and everybody else be free."

AMY: "Young girls have to know: Don't devalue yourself. No matter what you think right now, try not to compare yourself to people and try not to make some kind of weird judgment about yourself. Surround yourself with people who can tell you things."

ELIZABETH: "And that like you. And appreciate you."

AMY: "Find something about yourself that you can like, and you can love, so that you don't have to feel like you have to hide yourself or belittle yourself."

ELIZABETH: "Be authentic to yourself."

These are women who started very young themselves. In fact, they weren't allowed to participate in the very first pride march in Washington, D.C., because Elizabeth was too young. They, and BETTY, are two decades farther down the road now. One wonders: Have their dreams been fulfilled?

AMY: "I'm super lucky. I would like to have a bigger voice, that's all. I would like more people to know what we do. A bigger voice for the art, a bigger voice for change."

ELIZABETH: "My dreams have been fulfilled. I'm healthy, I have an amazing group of friends, I've been able to do what I want to do my whole life, and I see that continuing."

AMY: "We don't ever want it to end. We want it to continue. We want it to get a little easier—it's hard to be an independent artist."

ELIZABETH: "I have a roof over my head, enough food, I'm able to lend my voice to causes I believe in and help, and give money, and give time —and I have a great sister who I've spent my whole life with, although we're nemeses a lot of the time."

AMY: "She bugs me."

The secret of Amy and Elizabeth Ziff's success—and BETTY's, too—is a simple one. Life is about showing up. And these sisters know how to do that in spades.

Phyllis Lyon

Phyllis Lyon likes to tell a story that is alarming in the world of coincidence and close calls.

"Del proposed. And I said 'Well, I don't know, honey.' I said I wasn't sure I really wanted to settle down. I was here in San Francisco, and she went back to her job in Seattle. I puttered around and worried what to do about Del. Finally—and I don't know how long it was—I decided that this was ridiculous, and why *didn't* we get together? I drove out to the ocean, and I wrote her a letter saying OK. I sent it off to her. It turned out that she had been saying to a friend in Seattle that I wouldn't settle down, and her friend said, 'You know, why don't you just drop her? There's no reason to hang on.' Evidently I sent my letter right at the same time she was getting ready to write me.

"Del came down on a Greyhound bus and arrived about 11:00 P.M. on Valentine's Day, 1953. And there we were: two women who were very much in love, but very confused. But we were together."

And where would we all be without Del Martin and Phyllis Lyon?

If their names aren't familiar to you, their work probably is. This incredible couple set out on a path back in 1955 that likely changed every lesbian's life forever, by co-founding the first lesbian political group: The Daughters of Bilitis, or D.O.B. (Bilitis was a fictional contemporary of Sappho—a name purposely chosen for its obscurity.)

When Phyllis met Del in Seattle in 1950, she had no idea what a homosexual even was. She had graduated from the University of California at Berkeley, and had had some success as a newspaper reporter, partly, she points out, because most of the men who might have gotten the jobs then were off at war.

There were a bunch of women Lyon hung around with back then, and Del, a young divorcée, was new to the gang. "We joined the Press Club in Seattle and us girls would go over for drinks. This girl Pat, whom I was friendly with, and her friend Del went over for a drink. We ordered our martinis, and somehow got

on the subject of homosexuality. I can't imagine how. I didn't even know the word, and Pat didn't, so . . . guess who? Del was telling us all this stuff and one of us finally said, 'How do you know all this?' and Del said, 'Because I am one.' Our mouths dropped." Phyllis shakes her head. "I called all the women we worked with and told them. I had no idea it might be bad. I thought it was exciting, and I thought they would think so, too."

It wasn't long before Phyllis began to realize this was a subject best left under wraps. Still, she and Del became friendly, and when they traveled together to see their respective parents in San Francisco, Del would take her to the gay bars. "There were tons of bars. *Tons!*" she recalls. Of course the friendship eventually turned romantic, and the famous Valentine's Day finally took place.

It wasn't long after that that the young lovers found themselves looking for a new apartment—and suddenly considering a mortgage instead of renting a place. They had found a little house at the top of San Francisco's Noe Valley, with an incredible view down Castro Street and the entire city of San Francisco. "We stood and looked out the window and that was it. My mother came to look and said, 'There are no closets!'" But closets seemed to be one thing Del and Phyllis didn't need. "We decided we had to have it." Their home would become a place where a lot of political action over the next several decades either sprang from or took place. But at the time they bought it, they just

Just Doing It

 I don't think we thought about being out. We were not being open—but we were. I look back now and it's a miracle we didn't run into some problem. We were always together."

thought of it as a good party house, a great place for the newly formed D.O.B. meetings to take place.

"We just wanted to start a secret society where lesbians could get together and dance and have a drink, without fear of being arrested. The whole idea was to use peoples' houses. We had been here in our house only a few months—we had sleeping bags, a propane camp stove, a board-and-brick bookcase, and a Philco radio-phonograph."

It was Phyllis and Del who finally brought politics to the Daughters of Bilitis and made it what it was. They had already been active in Democratic circles in the area, and worried that the lack of employment and housing rights, especially, were going to be trouble for the burgeoning community of gays and lesbians suddenly walking hand in hand around the city. At this point, they lost a few of the D.O.B.'s apolitical members—but soon began to pick up even more.

They realized very early on that the small San Francisco meetings were not enough, and that the Daughters had to reach out to other women. "After a while, Del and I decided we had to do something more to let people know we existed. You couldn't put an ad in the paper—the only time anything gay and lesbian was in the paper was when somebody got arrested. So we decided we needed a newsletter. We weren't talking about the right to get married back then: What we wanted was the right to go to a bar and not get arrested, the right to not lose your job." So they started publishing *The Ladder*, and it changed lesbian politics forever.

"We had a desk in a corner of the Mattachine Society [a gay men's political group] office. We ran off about 160 newsletters—I think it was eight pages—but at that point we only had about twelve members. We got every member to send a copy to anyone they knew, anywhere, and Del and I also mailed it off to anyone we could think of. We didn't use any names in it. People got really excited. It wasn't just us—other people were working with us. The second issue had poems and whatnot. We heard about one woman in Washington, D.C., who wouldn't let *The Ladder* out of her house, so every month, everybody came over to her house to read it. I was the editor, and my pen name was Ann Ferguson. After about four issues, we killed off Ann Ferguson."

From then on, Del and Phyllis used their own names—*The Ladder* became a lifeline to lesbians all over the country, and Phyllis Lyon and Del Martin started to become heroines in the community. Phyllis and Del headed the D.O.B. for many years, and then continued to help lead countless fights, actions, and other organizations, including the National Organization of Women, which shunned lesbian members, thinking it would tarnish their reputations. In fact, Del Martin became the first lesbian member of their board of directors.

"It was so much fun," Phyllis says now. "I don't know what we would have done if we hadn't done what we did. We would have gotten bored with each other." She laughs. "We enjoyed it. We were younger, and didn't need sleep. We could gallop around, and drink, then go to sleep and start all over again."

To say this makes light of their work is a huge understatement, of course. But Phyllis shrugs it off. "We didn't feel brave—these were just the right things to be doing."

Though Lyon insists that she and Del never cared much about the marriage issue, insisting there were other, more important problems at hand, San Francisco mayor Gavin Newsom married them in California's first same-sex wedding among some very teary friends in 2008, just weeks before Del's death.

Two months, nine days; after all they'd been through, for fifty-six years together, that's how long Phyllis and Del were married.

And the little house in Noe Valley? It's chock a block with awards, photographs of the two of them with luminaries, rainbow flags, plaques, and all manner of tributes and thank-yous to Phyllis and Del. But when asked what her proudest accomplishment has been over the last decades, Lyon says without missing a beat, "Buying this house. I still don't know how we managed to scrape the money together. And it wasn't worth $11,000, either." And with that, she gazes out the picture window over the landscape that she and Del Martin changed so dramatically.

Randi Weingarten

One is tempted to say the following to parents everywhere—many of whom are conservative, or part of the religious right, or who simply squirm at the thought of their kids with a gay teacher: "Listen, America. Thank God this lesbian is taking care of all your children."

And why not? Because, indirectly, that's what Randi Weingarten does for a living, and she does a helluva job. She is the President of the American Federation of Teachers (AFL-CIO), which makes her, as she says she's often introduced, "the boss of all the teachers." ("Not so," insists Randi. She says, "They're all *my* bosses.") It also makes her the first openly gay person—man *or* woman—to be elected president of a national American labor union. Every day Weingarten seems to have on her mind the same goals she did when she first started in the teacher business: "My goal was that every single school should be a school where parents would want to send their kids, and where educators would want to work. You focus on low-performing schools and how to turn them around; you focus on the kids who are most vulnerable; and you focus on fighting fights about the budget."

Randi and her sister both knew from childhood exactly how hard teachers work: Their mother was one. "The house we grew up in always had papers stacked up all over the place. The only time that the table in the living room/dining area didn't have papers was when there was company coming. We thought teachers worked much too hard." (Randi's sister now works in intensive care pediatrics. It could be said that both sisters are in the kid business. It certainly could be said that they both also work too hard.)

Rarely does a child's family experience translate so clearly—and so successfully—into the person they become as an adult. A teachers' strike in the Nyack, New York, school system, where Randi's mother worked, surely left its mark on the entire family. With her father recently out of work, and her mother opting to fight for teachers' rights, this labor dispute was financially disastrous for the entire family.

"My mother was on strike in Nyack for what I think was six weeks, and subject in New York State to Taylor Law penalties," recalls Randi, "which meant a two-for-one penalty for every day you were on strike. They were on strike for fundamental fairness. It showed me the remarkable resilience of these ladies, who basically made up the Nyack teaching force, to fight for what was right. I think six or seven teachers, out of a 300-plus workforce, were the only ones who walked in. Everyone else stayed on the line for that long. A strike is always a tool of last resort, not of first resort, and essentially means that everything else has failed, because it is certainly a no-win situation for everyone. That strike showed me what the potential of collective action is against what was a truly horrible management that just wanted to break these ladies—their spines and spirits.

"Management thought it would be better," says Randi, "if they could force these women to hew to whatever line the administration wanted at that moment in time. What that strike did was make sure that people never went on strike again, including the school district never wanting there to be another strike. It created a level of peace that was necessary for both the teachers to be treated at least fairly and, most importantly, for the kids to be treated fairly and get a decent education."

Evidently, that was the handwriting on the wall for Randi Weingarten, though she couldn't have known it at the time. This relatively short period in her teenage years "dominated every part of our day," she recalls. "My experiences growing up were pretty informative in terms of the stuff that I'm doing now. I went to the Cornell School of Labor Relations, so I guess it impacted my life."

Randi continued on to law school, and worked for several years at Manhattan's Stroock & Stroock & Lavan, serving clients in—what else?—labor relations, eventually ending up as legal counsel at the United Federation of Teachers (UFT), the union for New York State. By 1998, she was their president. The fight was on.

Working in the Vortex

 Teachers make a difference in the lives of kids. To have the ability to work as both teacher and leader by working in the education labor union is a remarkable experience, because you are at the vortex between the two engines of social opportunity: the labor unions being the engine for working people and the public education system being the engine of opportunity for kids."

Basic to Weingarten's philosophy is that the needs of the teachers and the students are inseparable. "Teachers' lives and professional aspirations are completely intertwined with the achievement and success of their kids. One might argue that sometimes cities cannot afford to allow teachers the kind of economic dignity they deserve, but if the public has confidence in the school system, they will support the public schools." And she went on to prove it in her years at the UFT. The changes, especially in New York City, are legend— and by then, Randi knew what she was up against first-hand. She had spent six years as a teacher, part-time, full-time, and all the time at Clara Barton High School in Crown Heights, Brooklyn. Suddenly she had a whole new concern: that the kids would think she was a fraud. "Kids are different from adults," Weingarten points out. "They can figure out very quickly not just who cares about them, but who is real and who isn't, who knows their stuff and who doesn't, and who wants to help them and who doesn't." You can hear about poor school conditions, know about low teaching salaries, but seeing really was believing for Randi. Plus, she says, "Teaching taught me to be a good listener."

During Weingarten's tenure at the UFT, teacher salaries went up 43 percent in New York City; this brought their incomes nearer to what their compatriots were making in the suburbs. This pay raise also, within the course of about a year, changed the caliber of the teachers; 17 percent of the staff had lacked the basic certification to be teachers. Within a year, after the first big raise, that number dropped to 2 percent. And school conditions were abhorrent. "In the late eighties and nineties," Randi says, "there were many safety issues in a lot of schools; there were schools that still had coal-burning heating systems, exposed wiring, windows that didn't operate, and roofs that leaked; there were thousands and thousands of kids in classrooms in trailers who didn't have books that were up-to- date—they still cited Kennedy as president; we had to scrounge for chalk."

Much has changed since then. "Graduation rates are going up, the dropout rate is going down, test scores are going up, parents' satisfaction is up, buildings are better, teacher quality is better, teaching conditions are better, safety is better, and teacher salaries are better. It says a lot to a parent that the schools are clean, that there are no exposed wires, that there is a science lab, that we have materials, and that the teachers are far more respected."

Weingarten was somewhat of a hero to New York teachers, and at every UFT election, she won in a landslide. When she became president of the American Federation of Teachers, she actually did both jobs for a year before relinquishing the UFT title in 2009 and moving to Washington, D.C.

Somewhere along the way, the world began to realize that Randi Weingarten is a lesbian. This in a country where, at this writing, nearly thirty states allow a gay person—or someone perceived as being gay—to be fired from their job because of their sexual orientation. Having someone who is *gay* as "the boss of all the teachers"? Unlikely at best.

"At some point in my life I realized that I wasn't going to make a secret of my being a lesbian, and I never made it a secret nor did I talk about it." Weingarten finally quelled the gossip in 2007 by making two separate speeches—one at her synagogue, and another at an LGBT advocacy event. "As the head of a teacher's union, I thought it was very important to debunk the myths that sometimes arise when you see this kind of discrimination. We had lots of examples—I remember particularly when they attempted to fire two gay teachers. [The president of the union at that time] sat with those teachers and looked at the cameras and said, 'These are my members. They are great teachers, and I am not going to allow discrimination.' So whether it was racial, religious, or based upon sexuality, discrimination wasn't tolerated; that is who our union has been."

Asked how she would describe her job to a room full of third-graders, Randi replies without hesitation: "I would say that I work every day to make their lives better by fighting to make sure that they had the opportunity to do anything they wanted to do in life."

And if they decide to grow up and be teachers? It is likely that Randi Weingarten will be there to help make that the opportunity of a lifetime.

Hon. Christine Quinn

This is not an unusual way for New York City's City Council Speaker to start her day: an early walk with Sadie, a sand-colored shelter dog equipped with one very floppy ear; a drop-off with one of Sadie's friends for a day of fun, and a breakfast meeting at the venerable Moonstruck Diner on Manhattan's Ninth Avenue, where there is much neighborly chit chat. (Even though two burly security guys follow along, Madame Speaker is the boss of Sadie's poop bag.) She's a woman, she's a feminist, and she's a lesbian, but there's something about red-headed Christine Quinn that still screams "old-fashioned Irish pol." And that's meant in the best possible way.

It's several weeks before primary day, and Quinn is running for reelection for her City Council seat. Everyone on her staff is in overdrive, including her top volunteer, who has been with her from the start: Lawrence Quinn, her dad. He has an office in the basement of City Hall, and shows up most days to help any way that he can. "Lately he's been spending a lot of time at the headquarters calling voters," Chris reports. And evidently he has quite a sales pitch. "He says, 'If she is doing anything that you don't like, tell me, and I'll make her stop. You know, I'm her father.' It's very funny. And the way he phrases it is hilarious." Clearly Quinn *fille* gets a big kick out of this, and it's certainly garnered some good PR for her.

Christine Quinn is quick to note that she was born at the Babies Hospital at Columbia, although her parents had moved from Inwood in Manhattan to Glen Cove on Long Island well before her birth. ("I can actually say I was born in New York City," she says happily.) Her family and upbringing were textbook middle-class Irish: "My sister and I went to the parish school and Catholic high school because, according to my mother, that is what you had to do. There was no choice." Her mom was a social worker at Catholic Charities, and her dad was an electrical engineer and union shop steward. The only rough moment Chris remembers in her parents' marriage was that once, after a big fight, her mother stormed out of the house and went and changed her voter registration to the Republican Party, just to infuriate her husband.

What Chris did not know about her mother was that she was sick most of her daughter's young life. She died of breast cancer when Chris was sixteen, and though she was aware of the illness from around the eighth grade, she had cancer for several years before that. Her death was the single moment that Quinn says changed her life forever.

One of the difficult repercussions was that later on in life Chris had to come out to her father alone. "Our first conversation about it was not a good one. He said, 'You should never say that again.' But I think he realized he had a choice. He could cut off a relationship with his daughter, and I think that he made a decision, weighed the pros and cons in a fairly, probably scientific way, and decided it was not worth it. And then in doing that created the opportunity for everything to evolve."

Quinn's journey to accepting her homosexuality was not completely smooth, either. "In college I had an enormous crush on a woman. I remember going into my room and sitting down on the bed and thinking, out loud to myself, 'You've got enough going on. Enough challenges. You're not . . . This is not going to be one of them.'" In fact, when Quinn came to Manhattan and became campaign manager for openly gay City Council candidate (and now state senator) Tom Duane, he thought it was fascinating that Chris was straight, and would introduce her that way.

"I had kind of decided very consciously that I would have a great career; that I would be very successful;

that I would make an important impact and changes; and that I would not have a relationship. And that was fine." Quinn laughs and recalls, "I was dating men: extraordinarily sporadically and wildly unsuccessfully." When that changed, "Tom started to introduce me as his used-to-be-straight campaign manager."

It wasn't Tom Duane that first peaked Quinn's interest in politics, however. There were college internships in Hartford while she was at Trinity College, but she insists that it was the library at St. Patrick's Elementary School that sparked the fever.

"There was this flimsy little wire rack of paperbacks of important political people and important women . . . and I would read them till they were dog-eared. Just over and over and over again. People like the Kennedys, and Martin Luther King, Jr. I knew I wanted to work in politics, in social change, in activism. And I actually thought for a really long time that I did not want to be the elected official. Because

Eye on the Prize

 "You know, I am almost obsessed with the idea of doing more. Getting more done. Not looking back and feeling like there was anything I wanted to do that I didn't get done."

I thought, as the elected official, that you were one vote. And that it didn't really make sense to be one vote when you could be an organizer and potentially impact ten votes or fifteen votes or twenty or hundreds of votes. So it wasn't until I started doing tenant organizing in New York in the late eighties that I began to see that you could be an elected official *and* an organizer. And you could use the office in a way that was much more significant than one vote. It opened up my mind to being in electoral politics."

Chris was right. And it really works for her. Besides leading the fifty-one-member City Council, she is also still Chris Quinn from the neighborhood, responsible for her own district in Manhattan. Every waiter in the diner knows her, folks along the street wave, and she receives many knowing smiles during a walk along the High Line, the glorious public park née railroad that Quinn had championed since it was just a twinkle in local neighborhood dreamers' eyes. "The great thing about this city is that it is a series of *Mayberry RFD*s," she smiles, returning a wave.

Of course, she has also inevitably taken on responsibilities in many ways as New York City's "Head Gay." There is the annual tussle about New York's famed St. Patrick's Day parade, organized by the decidedly gay-unfriendly Ancient Order of Hibernians. Quinn has repeatedly refused to participate in the parade until the event's officials include LGBT Irish-American marchers. At this point, even wearing a pin or sash that would identify a participant as gay is not allowed.

On a larger scale, she speaks out frequently on LGBT issues, and leads rallies and marches in her home city and around the country. She speaks with vehemence—often referencing herself and longtime partner Kim Catullo—about gay civil rights: "Look me in the eye," Quinn will say, "and tell me I am less of a person than you are. Look me in the eye and tell me my family is worth less than yours."

Her views aren't popular with everyone, of course, but Chris stands by her outspokenness and her devotion to the job. "I do this type of work because I believe in it. So whenever there are dispersions cast about that it is just about pure ambition, or power. . . . " She pauses as she becomes emotional. "The best compliment I can get is that I am hardworking. And that I have been able to help people. "

No one doubts that Christine Quinn's political acme is still in the future. When queried as to what it would take for her dreams to come true, she ponders for just a moment and admits, "You know, I don't know. I think that if one comes true, I will just make another one."

Linda Villarosa

"**G**rowing up, I was what you'd call a 'good girl' . . . in high school I was a cheerleader, president of the senior class, captain of the track team, an honors student, and a prom queen candidate, and I still managed to work evenings and weekends. I had a nice boyfriend, and I wanted to marry him. . . . "

Coming out is difficult in the best of circumstances. Now, think about coming out in an article, written with your mother, in the magazine where you work. Gulp.

But that's just what Linda Villarosa did in *Essence* magazine back in 1991. And it earned her a lot of press, a lot of mail—some loving, some heartbreaking, some hateful—but more mail than any other article the magazine had ever published. Linda does not shy away from life.

The Villarosas were always a close family, and though it took Clara some time to come to terms with her daughter's sexuality, they had been through more trying times before. When she was ten, Linda's family packed it up in Chicago ("My father said, 'I can't take it anymore—I don't want to live with my in-laws forever") and decided, in true American fashion, to head west. Everybody got a say, including Linda and her sister, and the family started hunting for a new home.

"After visiting a lot of places, often being the only black family to be seen, we moved to Denver," Villarosa recalls. "This was the late sixties, early seventies. When we got this house in the suburbs—my parents had never had their own house, so they were so excited, they didn't really look at the neighborhood—we were the only black family. We hadn't moved in yet, we were staying in a motel, and we decided to just go visit and see it, because we were so excited. So then we're driving up and we see the neighbors up front scrubbing the garage door, because someone wrote 'niggers go home' on the garage. So the neighbors were upset and trying to scrub it off and they were so appalled. They said, 'This is not how we are, it's an isolated thing. We don't know what has happened.' They cleaned it off, and they moved us in with our stuff."

This wasn't the end of the story. "We had lived there for maybe two weeks when this man and his son came to the door. They're both in tears, crying, sobbing. The father says, 'Tell them! Tell them!' And the boy said, 'I wrote it on your garage!' This is our neighbor—I was in class with this kid. 'I'm so sorry I did this. My cousin talked me into it.' And the father said, 'Say it again, say you're sorry again!' So that was our welcome to Denver." Linda pauses. "Everything was much better from there."

Villarosa was just a kid when she first knew she wanted to be a writer. Her whole family was behind her, as usual. She remembers visiting relatives at their vacation home in Michigan. "My aunt and uncle always said, 'We know you're going to be a writer.' *Everybody* knew I was going to be a writer. They said, 'We picture you here, sitting in this beautiful house in the woods, writing.' My uncle was a drunk and burned down the house, so that didn't happen," Linda recalls with a laugh. But nothing else seemed to hold her back. "Writing came naturally," she shrugs.

Villarosa ended up at the University of Colorado, and took on a summer internship in New York. "So I came and worked for *Women's Day* magazine—it was my absolute last choice. I was very radical in college, I had a huge afro, I was going to work for the Peace Corps, go overseas, work for a clinic, work for radical newspapers, write a book about radical something." So no one was more surprised than Linda to find that she loved the fairly square monthly. Another magazine and a publishing house later and she found herself where she really wanted to be—at *Essence*.

It was the health editor job that had opened up, and that fed at last into Linda's desire to pursue public health. She has always been a fierce athlete, which really made the position fit her personality. "I had my own feelings about how to talk about health and how to educate people in print about health; I felt like I should really learn a little more, so I ended up at Harvard with a fellowship in public health for

journalists. That kind of got me where I could read studies much better. I understood health statistics, I understood the nuts and bolts, biology." And now Villarosa began to make some landmark changes.

"I wanted to write a book about environmental racism, but that was never going to sell. An agent came to me, and said 'Why don't you write the black woman's *Our Bodies, Ourselves?*' I was really very interested in African-American women's health, because it hadn't been done. And there were things that were different. So I really threw myself into that. And part of the reason I did that was it was very off-putting to read books where we were left out; a lot of those books, people were feeling like, this isn't for me, they were feeling angry. It's like, wait, this is insulting." The book was called *Body & Soul: The Black Women's Guide to Physical Health and Emotional Well-Being* and it sold hundreds of thousands of copies. Linda coauthored other health-related titles in the next few years: *Finding Our Way: The Teen Girls' Survival Guide* and *The Black Parenting Book: Caring for Our Children in the First Five Years.*

It was during this time that Linda and her mother Clara (who founded the famous Hue-Man Experience Bookstore in Denver, and later in Harlem) penned the "coming out" article in *Essence.* By now Linda was a senior editor there, and nervous about how the story might affect her career, worried there would be blowback from not playing the right part in the African-American women's community. "I thought, 'Don't come out here, you have just gotten to *Essence*, this

All for One

 I think that it is all one community. I think there are people who straddle the different communities, people like me, who can be ambassadors. I was talking to somebody who said, 'I don't want to educate people.' Well, I love to educate people, I want to educate people."

is your dream job, don't blow it, just fit in here.' So I didn't tell anybody. But there was a culture of revelation there; talking about yourself was highly valued." What she found, unexpectedly, was that "there was a tremendous outpouring of support, and also gratitude. I'd heard that kind of thing before, you know, you have to be the best kind of black, the right kind of black person, which I didn't like—that's ridiculous. And the definition of being the best kind of black or, as my cousin Tracy Scott Wilson's play is called, *The Good Negro*, is so narrow that there are only a few people who fit into it." Taking the high road was the right decision: Not long after, Linda Villarosa was made executive editor of *Essence* magazine.

Villarosa remained at the magazine until 2005, when full-time devotion to writing, teaching, and raising a son and a daughter with partner Jana Welch took over. There was another stop Villarosa needed to make along the way, however: *The New York Times*. Though HIV/AIDS had long been a pandemic, its crippling effect on the African-American community— especially on women—had not been adequately

chronicled. Linda took up the cause with a vengeance, becoming one of the nation's experts: Twice her groundbreaking articles appeared on the front page of *The New York Times*. And in 2008, Linda turned to fiction with her first novel, *Passing for Black*, which was nominated for a Lambda Book Award. (And yes, the subject of "the good negro" does play a part.)

All these accolades were appreciated, but make no mistake: This kind of reportage is life altering. "I've written about really hard things. I've written about sexual abuse, interviewed people who have abused, interviewed people who are living with HIV, who have died of AIDS, who are activists, who are doctors—you know, it's hard. There are a lot of hard places that I've gone to, and I've had to pull down that curtain a little, or else I'll be so emotional . . . I'm protecting myself, because I want to be able to write a story, I don't want to curl up and go to bed."

Though her radical afro has been replaced with long, luxurious dreadlocks, all of Linda Villarosa's radical thoughts still lie beneath the surface, lining up, one by one, and find their way, somehow, to the printed page.

Kate Kendell

"It's not every day that a good Mormon girl grows up and becomes a lesbian activist," Kate Kendell laughs ruefully. "It should happen a lot more—the world would be a much better place."

In fact, it's not every day the world finds a Kate Kendell, period—but sometimes heroines do spring from the most unusual places. Since 1996, Kate has been the executive director of the National Center for Lesbian Rights (NCLR), a legal organization committed to advancing the civil and human rights of lesbian, gay, bisexual, and transgender people and their families.

Kate's story is in many ways what lots of kids face growing up: learning how to reconcile what you've been told is right and true by your parents and by your church with what you feel in your heart. In Kendell's case, that involved a beloved and religious mother and Mormonism, a religion that, in the state of Utah, is so prevalent that it seems to be more than just a church, but a culture.

"I was devout as a kid," Kendell recalls. "I went to church every Sunday because that's what everybody did. I was involved in the church and all the extracurricular stuff, because that was the social life for almost every kid.

I wouldn't say I was ever a true believer. There were moments of spiritual depth that I think you can have in any kind of setting where you're trying to be your best self. . . . All religions try to do that. I had moments of transcendence that made me feel an allegiance to the church because I felt that they were tied to the church."

But Kate knew she was a lesbian fairly early on, and the life choices began. "I fell in love with my Mormon camp counselor. To this day, we are close friends, and I truly believe that she saved my life. If I had not met her, I probably would have done what was expected of me: I would have gotten married to a man, had children, gotten divorced, and would have then needed the NCLR to get custody of my kids. I was seventeen, she was thirty. She was married at the time—it was a complicated and difficult situation to navigate." Kate's understanding of a heterosexist society came early because of this first relationship. "Forced heterosexism: She got married because that's what you were supposed to do. If people didn't get married because that's what society expected of them, we'd save a lot of marriages and we'd save a lot of kids from the trauma of parents who never should have gotten married in the first place." Though she didn't know it at the time, the seed of much of NCLR's work was planted in her consciousness.

Kate's serious misgivings about the church came to a head during college. "I discovered feminism. That's why I left the church. I was transformed by the feminist writings I was exposed to in college, and I just thought, 'I can't be a Mormon and a feminist.' I found it quite easy

to leave the church—I had one foot out already if I look back. I asked a professor of mine who was a Mormon and a self-identified feminist: 'How do you do it? How do you manage to be a feminist and a Mormon?' And he said, 'Well, the church needs us. We need to make change from within. We need to have the church do better on issues of feminism and inclusion.' And I thought, 'Well, maybe you can do that because you're a white guy. You've got a lot of privilege in the church, and you don't have to give up any of that privilege to be a feminist. But I do. I didn't have any angst over leaving the church.'"

After graduating from the University of Utah College of Law, Kate spent some requisite time at a big Utah law firm. After a couple of years, she realized that it wasn't the position for her, but being a staff attorney at the Utah American Civil Liberties Union (ACLU) was. "I loved every day of it. I loved the variety. The ACLU is consistently rated the most hated organization in Utah, so it was a total blast," she recalls with a wicked smile. It must have seemed like perfection, but soon Kendell had a long-distance girlfriend in San Francisco, and there was a job open at NCLR. So she arrived on the West Coast, where she served for two years as legal director before taking the reins.

NCLR has changed quite a bit since its founding in 1977, and Kate has seen a lot of it. Donna Hitchens and Roberta Achtenberg were young lawyers when they started what was then called the Lesbian Rights Project. "Lesbians were losing custody of their kids right and left coming out of heterosexual marriages.

And no one was doing anything about it. In fact, when Donna graduated from Berkeley Law School, she knew Del Martin and Phyllis Lyon (longtime lesbian activists and Daughters of Bilitis cofounders), and they brought her a folder of stories that they had heard over the years from lesbians who had lost their children." Phyllis and Del always had a listed phone number, and it served as almost an early lesbian hotline. "They gave the folder to Donna and said 'You have to fix this.'

"Very quickly, they realized the rising tide lifts all boats—and if there were men that were losing custody of their kids due to their sexual orientation and we could win on their behalf, that helps not only gay men, but it helps lesbians, too. One of the first famous cases NCLR took on was a gay man who lost custody of his son to his ex-wife, who had taken the boy to live with a religious cult in Texas." Achtenberg represented him; NCLR's budget was about $30,000—the cost of the case about $200,000. They raised the money, and NCLR won.

Since then, the organization's work has centered on issues such as adoption, immigration law, elder law, and youth projects. How do they know what

Fighting It Out

 The reason that NCLR is still needed is that we've been flexible enough to morph and to continue to ask the question 'Are we relevant?'

NCLR needs to be next? "We check in with Donna and Roberta and with Phyllis Lyon constantly, and some of our longtime donors. 'We're thinking of doing this, what do you think?' we ask them. 'Is that who we are?' The bottom line, Kendell says, is always, "Who's still not getting their issues addressed? Who's left behind? And *bam*, that's where we're going."

NCLR also led the legal battle for the repeal of Proposition 8 to retain gay marriage laws in the 2008 California elections (a particularly tough pill for Kate Kendell to swallow, since the Mormon Church took the lead on passing it). Kate had married her longtime partner Sandy Holmes during the brief time California permitted marriage; they have two children, and Kate has a daughter from a former relationship. Her fury remains unabated. "The constitution either means what it says, and that's the end of it, or we're going to willy-nilly decide who gets protected and who doesn't simply by who's in favor and who's out."

But she is ever-confident, especially when speaking of the future of the LGBT movement. "I think every-one knows the end of the story—there's no doubt in my mind how it ends. It ends with LGBT people protected under the law, able to marry, fully included in civil soci-ety. Now, just like with race, there will still be racism, there will still be bigotry, there will still be moments of indignity, but formal law will recognize us. The question is: That's the end chapter; how many more chapters first? That remains to be seen." Just don't be surprised to find Kate Kendell there, closing the book.

Dr. Susan Love

She is adamant. She is kind. She is adamant. She is funny. But oh, she is adamant.

What she is adamant about is eradicating breast cancer, and she is determined to do it in her lifetime. Her name is Dr. Susan Love, and if you are a woman or a man in America, it's almost certain that she has touched the life of someone you know.

Most of the world began to know Dr. Love's name when her first book, *Dr. Susan Love's Breast Book*, appeared in 1990. It set the medical community on its ear, and it opened hundreds of thousands of women's eyes to the truth about breast cancer. It sounds simple now to hear Love say, "It became clear to me that I knew how to talk to women." It was anything but simple. "Doctors hated it," she flatly declares, "because it was the first book that explained the science to the public, and doctors really thought I was telling secrets."

If she sounds like a bit of a rabble-rouser, a maverick, perhaps even a thorn in people's side, well, she is—and proud of it. Susan Love has a nicer way of putting it: "I'm a catalyst." But any corporation would be thrilled to have

her in their boardroom—she devises an agenda, she believes in it wholeheartedly, and she'll move heaven and earth to push it through.

This can't all come from her previous incarnation as a nun . . . can it?

In many ways, yes. Before the *Breast Book*, before the Dr. Susan Love Research Foundation, before the Love/Avon Army of Women, there was a vocation, a calling. It's simply how her mind — and her heart — works. The first path Susan Love followed was a religious one, fraught with doubts almost from the first. Though Susan was born in New Jersey, the Love family moved to Puerto Rico, where Susan spent many of her elementary school years. "When I went to school in Puerto Rico," she explains, "I was the only one in my class who was primarily English-speaking. Except for the nuns. So I identified more with the nun thing. So if you even think about being a nun, that's God telling you you should be one. If it even enters your brain, that's the Holy Spirit. It's a vocation." So after two years at a Catholic college, she joined a convent in Connecticut. "They sent me to Fordham University—in a habit. It was right after Vatican II and nobody in the convent knew what they were doing." These were chaotic times in the Catholic Church—Pope John Paul II had relaxed many centuries-old rules, from no-meat Fridays to mass in the vernacular to nuns in mufti.

"The nuns knew that the rules were changed, but they didn't know what they were going to be. It was a very confusing time. Before taking your own name and [wearing] no habits, it had been scrubbing the floors and praying all the time. Now they had a weekend of psychological testing to see if we could actually live in community life.

"I went to Fordham in clothes first, and I found it too hard to allegedly be a nun in clothes on a college campus. It was very awkward—I was a junior now—so I asked for the habit. At least if I had the habit on, people treated me like I was a nun, and it was easier to try to be one. And it was the middle of the sixties! I agonized and agonized about becoming a nun. I worried that I was too prideful and all that crap. My mentor from high school said to me, 'Is this making you crazy?' And I said yes, and she said 'Well, then leave. God doesn't want you to be crazy.' So I left the convent, finished at Fordham, then applied to go to medical school. The nuns were going to send me. They had this whole idea I was going to take care of all the old sick nuns."

One is tempted to quote the old adage here: "Right church, wrong pew." Susan Love knew by now that she wanted to help people, but realized she was going about it the wrong way. The bottom line for her? "They wanted to save souls; I wanted to save the world."

Now Susan Love's life began in earnest, and surprisingly, the law, not religion or medicine, is what gave her a jump start. "It started with Title IX for me," she says, "which was in 1972. What people don't realize about Title IX is that it wasn't about sports at first. Any school that takes federal money cannot discriminate. It went from a 5 percent quota to no quota, so admissions went from 5 percent to 30 percent for women's admissions in medical schools in one year.

"We had to be better than the guys—we had to be better than the guys to get in in the first place. It became sex-blind like that," Love recalls, snapping her fingers. "So I applied to all these med schools and my college adviser said, 'If you go to med school you will kill some boy. Because he'll have to go to Vietnam.' If he went to med school, he'd get a deferment. If I took his place, he'd have to go get shot."

Love finished near the top of her class, but the discrimination had just started for her.

"So the guy who's the chief of surgery asks me what I want to do and I say I want to become a surgeon. 'Not in my program. I don't believe women should be surgeons,' says he. So I went to Beth Israel in Boston. I was the second woman surgeon in the training program there; I was the first woman ever on the staff at Beth Israel as a general surgeon. I was the second woman chief resident. My life has been a fight," admits Love. "It always has. It still is, in some ways.

"I went out in general practice, and I said, 'I'm not going to let them make me be a breast surgeon. God forbid you be allowed to do the macho surgery—which I was perfectly capable of doing, godammit. The only patients anyone referred to me were women with breast problems. That's the only way you get patients when you start out: referrals.

"I would spend a lot of time explaining things to women: what their disease was, how it worked, what the options were—which nobody else did! And it was amazing. Before I knew it, I had this busy practice. Other doctors were trying to figure out why I was stealing all their patients from them. What they didn't get is that we were talking to people like intelligent human beings. The guys had been taking care of the surgery

We're Not Getting Older, We're Getting Better

 Look at Hillary Clinton and what she's doing. Gloria Steinem! Look at Madeleine Albright! People who just went out there and did it. And they weren't young. I think we get better as we get older. With the menopause thing: I say we need high levels of hormones to domesticate us enough that we'll reproduce the race, and then we get liberated from them with menopause. And then we regain our power, and we can take over the world."

for so long, and it was always 'don't worry your pretty little head about it, we'll take care of it, dear.' You'd go under for the surgery, half the time you didn't know if you were going to wake up with a breast or not."

It was during this same time, in the early 1980s, that Love met her now-wife, Helen Cooksey. Susan had been on what she calls a find-a-man campaign with another colleague when Cooksey, who was on staff with her, asked Susan to spend a weekend with her at her cabin. "I knew she was gay, and I thought she was very scary. On some level I thought it was catching, and I was right—she *was* contagious!" They have been together since that weekend, and have a daughter, Katie. Never doing things halfway when they could be breaking barriers, Susan and Helen won the first second-parent adoption case in Massachusetts. "It was hard to say we weren't fit," Love says wryly.

In her work, Love was beginning to realize that "the climate was just right: It was after the AIDS epidemic had hit, women's lib had happened, and people were beginning to think about breast cancer and whether we should politicize it. I called all the groups together that were starting up, and we started the National Breast Cancer Coalition in 1991. In the first year or two, we managed to increase the money for breast cancer research from $90 million to $300 million. I said to Helen, 'I'm the exact person that has to do it. The survivors trust me because of the book, but the powers trust me because I'm a doctor. I can straddle those two things.' And I knew that it had to be run by the women

with breast cancer—which it is. I'm really good at catalyzing and then getting out of the way."

And now she's done it again, by partnering the Dr. Susan Love Research Foundation with Avon to start the Love/Avon Army of Women. This is no rah-rah group of cheerleaders, no mere wearing of the pink ribbon. The Army—which is aiming for a million "soldiers"—signs up women with and without breast cancer who will agree to volunteer for myriad research studies.

Now, here's where the adamant Dr. Susan Love comes in. "If you mobilize people and focus on what causes breast cancer, you can cure it. You have to give people the vision that this is a doable thing. If you focus and you put in the money and you work on it, you can get there."

"If you look at breast cancer in a Westernized country, the average age for a woman with breast cancer is sixty-four: it's a post-menopausal disease," Love points out. "In the underdeveloped nonwestern countries? It's all premenopausal. The average age is forty-eight. In the African American community? It's all premenopausal. That premenopausal disease? That's a virus. I guarantee you."

Dr. Susan Love puts it even more simply: "The key to ending breast cancer is to learn how to stop it before it starts."

The troops are lining up, the march is on, and if her past tells us anything, Dr. Susan Love has ideas brewing that will, once more, change forever the way women live.

Nan Buzard

Nan Buzard isn't someone you see on the nightly news. But turn on your TV and you do see the terrible things man and nature offer up that make her work a never-ending battle of trying to put the world back together again, or at least trying to make it inhabitable.

Buzard laughingly calls herself an "International Do-Gooder." It's a good description, and if it has the ring of a superhero, then so be it. Her paycheck actually comes from the American Red Cross, where she is currently the senior director of International Response & Programs, but her office is in whatever part of Africa, Asia, or Latin America is in need.

It almost seems like Nan had service in her DNA. That, and water. Buzard and her partner presently live on a houseboat in a marina in Washington, D.C., with a view of the Washington Monument and official-looking helicopters buzzing overhead. Her father was a sailor who left her and her mother when Nan was a few months old. Mother and child moved to a small Hudson River town overlooking a boatyard. When she was twelve, her mother moved to Costa Rica to run a hotel, and Nan headed off to boarding school.

"The schools I attended were Quaker and were all on farms in rural areas. The main orientation of these schools was service: service to community, service to each other, with a lot of farming activity and taking care of neighbors. It was drilled into me early on."

It was also during this time that Buzard came out, barely ruffling anyone's feathers—including her own. "I actually thought I was supposed to be a monk or a nun because I couldn't understand what I was supposed to do with myself. I didn't know what my place was. I didn't have crushes the way other people had crushes; my crushes were on girls all the time. But once I figured it out, it was easy. 'Oh, I'm gay. Of course that's what it is.' It was like a big shot of sunlight—fabulous!—and I proceeded to tell everyone in my life. I didn't sleep with anyone and didn't have a girlfriend until at least two years later. But it still felt great coming out. It wasn't about sleeping with anyone; it was about recognizing who and what I was."

One of Nan's first work experiences was a job at the Oscar Wilde Memorial Bookshop in New York's Greenwich Village, the world's first gay bookstore (which closed its doors after forty years in 2009). Craig Rodwell, once Harvey Milk's lover, still owned it at the time.

"Oscar Wilde was really the only place for gay people to congregate—there was no Gay and Lesbian Community Center—and everyone came through there. For example, there was an attack on gay men; a crime called the Ramrod Shooting where a guy drove by and shot all of these men dead. There was a lot of really, really bad stuff going on and people would call the bookstore because there was no other place to contact. There were no gay hotlines, so it was 'the center,' and we were exposed to all of the horrors that happened to gays and lesbians and all the wonderful parts of our community. So it was a very nurturing, inspiring, and enraging place to be, because you saw the whole pantheon of what happens to gays.

"That decade from the late seventies to the late eighties was pivotal in terms of the number of lesbian and gay service groups that came to be: I was in Dykes Opposed to Nuclear Technology; Dykes Against Racism Everywhere; Lesbians Against Sexual Taboos; it was a rich ferment and almost everything started back then. I felt a great need for service—and after almost fifteen years of it, I began to feel almost ghettoized."

But it was a vacation that spun Buzard around and gave her direction. "I took a trip for six months around Africa and remember coming back to my little apartment on East Fifth Street—a fourth-floor walk-up, nothing special—and I remember walking in, closing the door behind me and locking it. I turned on the light, went to the sink and washed my hands, and thought how I'd just spent six months where people had no doors to close or locks to protect themselves. They had no lights to turn on. I remember feeling how powerful it is simply to have a door that you can lock and be safe; how extraordinary it is to be able to turn on a light and illuminate darkness; how amazing it is to be able to wash your hands. Think about people with no doors, just plastic sheeting; think about the women and children and their vulnerability; think about having no light; not being able to read and not having any opportunity to get an education."

It took her a couple of years to find her "place," but she ended up at a small nongovernmental organization, and then got recruited to help run the 1995 United Nations World Conference on Women in Beijing.

"I did work at the United Nations for a while, for the UN Refugees Agency, which I thought was a very good and important agency," Nan recounts. "Why the Red Cross? Because I found it to be the best vehicle for me to do the humanitarian work I want to do. The Red Cross for me is about the immediacy of responding to people in need. The mandate, the core mission of the Red Cross, is disaster response and alleviating suffering. For those of us who sometimes don't have great confidence in long-term solutions even though we know that they are critical, it's the immediacy of trying to alleviate some of that suffering, the immediacy of providing different services that address that immediate need."

Nan ticks off the places she's worked over the years, and it's stunning in its tragedy: Sierra Leone, Afghanistan, Zimbabwe, East Timor, Haiti, Indonesia, and Bosnia-Herzegovina. She spends much of her time now living in Geneva, but emphasizes that her "real work at the American Red Cross is to make sure that the money we get from a very generous American public is to make sure that we steward it well, that

Taking Gayness to the Straight World

 One of the reasons I started doing international work was that I felt it was far more valuable for me to take my comfort and enthusiasm for being a lesbian into the straight world. It didn't have the kind of meaning, relevance, and need in the queer world. So for me it was like, OK, I am so happy being out, so comfortable being out, and I *like* being out—let me go be out in the straight world, not in the gay world. We laugh at National Coming Out Day, but it works. What changes the world? Knowing someone who is gay. There is so much truth to the statement 'One gay at a time.'"

we spend it efficiently, in the right place, and that as much money as possible gets to the people who need it most. And it is *work*."

Nan misses the early days of her fieldwork, and hopes to return to it soon. And she speaks to the future of the American Red Cross and other agencies. "I think that the bulk of the money needs to go to disaster risk reduction. That is working with communities—whether rural or urban—and asking, 'What is your greatest risk?' We also try to put our time and orientation into funds toward disaster preparedness so that people don't lose as much, it doesn't cost as much, they don't suffer as much. We all have to be thinking in that direction."

To some, this all sounds very valiant—and occasionally may induce a little guilt. Buzard wants to set that straight. "I don't want to make people feel guilty for what they're *not* doing. What I want people to understand is that there is an urgent need out there and there are a lot of different ways to serve. We felt this way as part of being gay: You can be an activist or you can give money to activists. It's not like there is only one way to serve."

Maybe it's having the Washington Monument out your aft porthole. Maybe it's the feeling you have to stand at attention every time a helicopter flies over. Or maybe Nan Buzard lives in sight of these things because that's the way she was built. If that's so, somebody needs to build more Nan Buzards.

Hilary Rosen

Hilary Rosen is tough. Anyone who's hired her, worked beside her, or tangled with her knows that. Hilary has been a lobbyist, an activist, a political mover and shaker, and a television commentator. She has never wanted to be a politician, but if you think that's because she believes they're on the wrong side of the law, you need to hear about Rosen's soft spot for America's elected officials: "I really admire politicians. I'd be that small 3 percent in the poll, in the national poll, about your perception. I think that they have very hard jobs; I think they take them because they're committed to change, and public policy, and doing good for people. I vehemently disagree with many of the policies of my Republican friends, but I don't doubt their commitment. I think the overwhelming majority of people in Washington involved with politics actually care about their role."

Oh, Hilary is full of surprises. One tends to think of the beginning of her visibility as a strong voice at the Human Rights Campaign Fund, though by the time she made her mark there, she had already been a staple on Capitol Hill—and a tagalong at her mother's side.

Growing up in suburban West Orange, New Jersey, Hilary virtually got the political bug at her mother's knee. "My mom was a politician: She was the first woman elected to our City Council. She took a fairly traditional path to elected office for women in those days, starting as a PTA volunteer, then PTA president, and then went for elective office. I kind of tagged along with her. I learned a lot about engagement from her.

"She was on the Democratic National Committee, so a lot of politicians would come to the house, and I would go with her to meetings all the time from a very young age. I remember her putting me on the phones for George McGovern in 1972, so I ran Students for McGovern for our county. I think that was the first campaign where I had an actual responsibility of my own." Rosen was fourteen years old.

Only a few years later, Hilary headed off to George Washington University, and perhaps the shock of her life—that she was a lesbian. She admits that it took her quite a while to feel comfortable in her own skin. "I fell in love with my roommate in college. That's my whole coming-out story. We were assigned to the same room freshman year because they assigned rooms alphabetically. Me, Dorie, and a girl named Susan." Rosen pauses to think. "After about six months, Susan moved out.

"I was shocked to fall in love with a girl," she recalls. "I didn't want to be gay. I thought it would be the killer of my ambitions, and it just didn't fit with my plans for myself. And yet I knew that I was, and

I was compelled to be, and so I struggled a lot. I was completely uncomfortable being gay for, I would say, the first seven or eight years—well into my twenties. I wasn't ever particularly closeted; I just didn't want to be gay myself. I think my self-acceptance really turned around during the AIDS crisis, because I finally realized that my internal shame was based on external prejudice." Maybe that's what it takes to make a good activist: the realization that the world you live in has no place for you, and that the only way to fit in is to change the game.

Hilary was mulling over her future, which she had decided would be a career in business, when life's next step fell in her lap. At the time, the only business she was pursuing was bartending.

"I was staying up late, getting in all sorts of trouble. The governor of New Jersey at the time was a friend of the family—he didn't think tending bar was a very nice job for a young lady, so he put me to work in his Washington office, and I started to focus on policy. And that was interesting. And it was a heady time because I was a kid and the governor was friends with the president, so he'd come to Washington and take me to the White House with him. I'd go meet with senators with the boss of the office and it was really interesting." Rosen had, by a fluke, discovered her strength early: "I loved lobbying. It is a very interesting mix of the personal and policy and figuring out how your particular need comes into play with the nation's needs at the time. What good lobbyists do, it

AIDS, Media, and the Movement

 AIDS was clearly my entry into gay politics. And what was so true about the AIDS crisis was how much of it was an outgrowth of the prejudice toward gay people— and gay men in particular—at the time. So for those of us who got involved then, I just think it empowered millions. And it radicalized closeted gays and gays who were out but hadn't done anything, because we were outraged at the lack of government attention. And I think it was also the first time where I saw the power and limits of the media when it comes to politics."

becomes less about the issue and more about really understanding how the process works." Fortunately for the LGBT community, Hilary's passion and talents were recognized by Vic Basile, the very first executive director at the Human Rights Campaign Fund [now the Human Rights Campaign (HRC)]. "He hired me to be HRCF's first contract lobbyist," Rosen recalls. "That was a proud moment."

Life was changing fast. In no time, our reluctant lesbian had realized the community's need and she became a full-on activist. She left HRCF's employ and soon became co-chair of their board of directors. (Hilary would return to HRC one more time, as interim executive director in 2004.) This coincided with a new job opportunity that would rock her world—and the whole of the music industry. Hilary Rosen went to work for the Recording Industry Association of America (RIAA).

What none of us knew then—and are all too aware of now—is that the recording business was headed for the most tumultuous years in its history. During those years, Rosen was at the helm of the RIAA, bringing the little-known trade group into the spotlight as its chairman and CEO. She looks upon that time as some of the best years of her working life.

"I just loved the music business. It was fascinating. I loved the crazy people I worked with and for, and I loved the variety of issues we worked on. I was deeply engrossed in how the technological changes were forcing new ways to think about the business.

And it was . . . it was a crazy and difficult time. It was as professionally fulfilling as you can imagine." Rosen adds, with a laugh, that this wasn't her first foray into the biz. "I worked at a Sam Goody music store in high school!" But it was her years of lobbying on Capitol Hill that brought many a victory to the RIAA, the recording industry, and performers alike.

Hilary's years of experience stating her position face-to-face with legislators finally went public: She began to appear as a popular political commentator on television. First on CNBC, then MSNBC, and finally, during the 2008 presidential election excitement, she signed on at CNN. She is former Editor-at-Large at *The Huffington Post*, and managing director at the Brunswick Group, an international public relations and communications strategy firm.

But for proudest moments, Hilary refers to two things: helping to procure the first AIDS-drugs money as a young lobbyist in 1983, and bringing up twins Anna and Jacob with former partner Elizabeth Birch. And after all these years of fighting the good fight, Rosen is perhaps surprisingly more upbeat than ever.

"I'm not so grumpy about the world. I'm an analytical optimist. I think that most of the world is a pretty great place and most people are pretty wonderful and accepting and want to do the right thing. I think that we don't have to succeed by playing victim. We can feel personally empowered and personally good about our place in the world, and still justify demanding equal treatment."

With Hilary Rosen on our side, we are well on our way.

Lupe Valdez

"How you doing?" "Hey, hi." "Did you put in a good day's work for me today?" It's shift change, and Lupe Valdez is greeting the steady stream of deputies on their way out, heading home. Almost everyone gets the "good day's work" question. There are lots of handshakes, the occasional clap on the back, and a heartfelt, "Yes, ma'am," from every single officer. It's enough to make an old-fashioned feminist weep.

Lupe Valdez is a rock star here: She's the sheriff of Dallas County. She has 2,600 people working under her, and it feels like we've just greeted half of them.

This is Texas, where being sheriff (sounds like "shurf" when Valdez says it) really means something. It's not exactly the Wild West in this gigantic urban sprawl, but the four stars on her collar get big-time respect here; they stand for something righteous and true. Even Valdez's boots get in on the action: Handmade and navy blue (to match her uniform), they sport the sheriff's five-pointed star on the front, and the state of Texas on the back. The left boot

boot sports SHERIFF in red leather, the right, VALDEZ. Very cool.

Valdez made waves from the get-go. This wasn't exactly the kind of sheriff that Dallas County had bargained for. Having a Democrat elected is surprise enough (she unseated a five-time Republican incumbent), but a woman? A Latina? A *lesbian*? It was a spotless career in positions as varied as county jailer, army captain, and federal agent for U.S. Customs and the Department of Homeland Security that brought her to the improbable position she holds today.

"This was a good-old-boy network," Valdez admits. "I'm so proud of Dallas County that they saw that and that they said, 'We need new blood.' I was an outsider." Valdez believes she was voted in on merit, and though her first term saw plenty of nasty nay-saying, she breezed through a second term election with a 10 percent lead in 2008. In fact, much of her first-term success had to do with her jail reform—something she knows from the inside—and cleanup in both the figurative, and much too literal, sense. Besides being desperately understaffed, the Dallas County Jail's bathrooms and prison walls were constantly covered with excrement, and about 1,000 inmates were sleeping on the floor. But now the press no longer refers to the jail's conditions as "third world." In fact, experts from big cities around the country have come to see how she's gotten it done.

Departmental corruption and low morale were next on the list. Though her personal profile was certainly unusual for Dallas, "being a federal agent helped a lot," she recalls. "There was a certain group that had all the privileges around here. And that group would use everything they could to throw at me—in the media, meetings, everything. But I honestly believe that the majority of people want to do the right thing, and they want to do what they're supposed to do. Once I got here I made a couple of changes. For promotions, I got rid of the inside interview board and got an outside vendor who could only see a number; they couldn't see the race, the height, weight, or anything else personal about the applicant. Minority promotions went up 23 percent in the first twelve months. I joked and said, 'I don't think they got that intelligent in such a short time.' We're just not recognized."

No one would know that better than Lupe Valdez. Born the youngest of eight children in San Antonio to a family of migrant farmworkers, Lupe was picking crops—albeit half-heartedly—by the time she was three. ("If you're not being carried, you work," is the unwritten rule.) Her mother was insistent that she be educated—though that didn't include college. People started urging Lupe to bus herself across town to a better high school. "It took me a while to realize that, on rainy days, I was the only one at school with muddy shoes. Our side of town did not have sidewalks or paved roads." But when she announced her decision to go to college, her father laid down the law. "'Women from our family do not go to college,' he

Coming Out to God

"Spirituality was very important to me. I used to run five or six miles a day, and I would start running and pray the whole time: 'OK, now I know what these feelings [of being a lesbian] are. You've got to take them away from me. If I'm supposed to be close to you, and keep my spirituality, then you've got to take these feelings away.' Then one day I read about something called the Metropolitan Community Church. And I remember there was a male couple with two little twin girls in their Easter bonnets and dresses sitting in front of me, and I kept thinking, 'There's something wrong here! How can these people be OK with God?' But when these two guys and their little girls were kneeling at the altar for Communion, I was behind them in line, and I remember saying 'Oh, my God, where have you been?' I only said it just above a whisper, but the woman in front of me in line turned around and said, 'We've been here, waiting for you.' That's when it made it OK for me."

insisted. It was, 'My house, my rules.' So I said, 'OK, no more your house—I'm leaving.' So I had to leave home in order to continue my education."

Valdez was puzzled by this, and more so decades later when she got no support when she decided to run for sheriff. "My family was ashamed of me running for sheriff. [Back when we were growing up], there were literally railroad tracks that you had to cross. We lived in this neighborhood, and you could only go across them safely during the day. I found

out when my dad died—he never shared this with me—that several times, because of work, they were caught on the wrong side of the tracks after dark, and their encounters with law enforcement were not very pleasant. My uncle was the one who told me: They got stopped, and were asked for their ID. They were citizens, of course, but the police were trying to make them illegal, so they handed over their identification and the officers—one of them was Latino, and this is why my dad was so upset, because he kept saying,

when you join them professionally, you become like them—threw their IDs on the floor and my uncle said, 'I handed it to you, and I would hope you'd hand it back the same way.' He shouldn't have said that. They got beat up pretty badly, because my uncle was being disrespectful to the officers. They literally just dumped them over the tracks. It wasn't that my father was angry at me. It was that he knew he couldn't help me. 'If you go *there*, I can't help you. If you cross the tracks, I can't help you.'"

Maybe that's why—consciously or not—Lupe Valdez's goal is always to help, one way or another.

She escaped to a self-imposed retreat before she decided to run for sheriff—something she likes to do when she needs to mull over big decisions. "I had three questions," she recalls. "Can I mentor? Can I make a difference? Can I influence?" Obviously, her answers were, "Yes, yes, yes," as was the voting public's. Even today, when asked about her plans for the future (because believe it, Lupe Valdez is far from done), her answer is fast and firm: "My plan is to turn this department around."

She's turned other lives around, too, far away from the sheriff's office. Valdez still mentors a high school student, and frequently meets people who want to thank her for her courage to change. She cites a woman she sat with on a plane ("white, conservative, Republican, with a football coach for a husband") who gushed about how thrilled her family was when Lupe won the election. "She teared up and said, 'My son is gay. We thought we were going to lose him. I love all my children, but my gay son is so wonderful. And you validate him.'"

It's this kind of thing that clearly keeps Lupe Valdez running, and speaks to her philosophy, which she signs herself up for every New Year's Day as her annual resolution: "To be a better person than the one I was the year before." Lesbian, Latina, or lawman—it's not a bad plan.

Elizabeth Birch

"I conspired to leave home from the time I was twelve."

This sounds like bad-girl talk; like the way a renegade, a miscreant, acts out. And if you've ever seen Elizabeth Birch suited up at a podium—speaking as executive director of the Human Rights Campaign (HRC), at the Democratic National Convention, or anywhere else—it seems almost ludicrous. To look at her, to listen to her, she appears to be to the corporation born. But the truth is, Elizabeth Birch *did* have the heart of a rebel: She ran away with the circus.

"I left home young because I was gay," states Birch, and nearly everything that has followed in her life since unfolds from that statement. She is the daughter of a Canadian Air Force pilot who spent her childhood living in various places—Vancouver Island, Alberta, Winnipeg, Ontario—as one of five bright children with a Great Santini figure for a father. "We all escaped, and we were all somehow ravaged by alcohol growing up." By the time Birch was eleven, she understood she was gay. Some kids merely know they're different, but Elizabeth understood what a lesbian was, though it would be several years before she actually met one. So soon the planning began for her. "I spent

every crack and crevice of my mental energy figuring how to get out." By the time she was fifteen, she had joined a carnival. By seventeen, she was gone for good. In between was a foray with a group that changed her life forever: Anyone who went to high school in the sixties and seventies will remember them as Up with People.

Up with People changed her life—perhaps, Birch says, even saved it. "I met what everyone would think was a schmaltzy, fake, inauthentic, right-wing group that came and sang and danced their way into our hometown. I fell in love with them. Up with People were all kids like me. It was chock-full of homosexuals, kids from the projects, draft dodgers, kids just trying to find themselves. We were totally the opposite of how Up with People presented themselves. We were communists and poets and beatniks and hippies."

Still, it was at this time Elizabeth first fell in love—it's also how she ended up living in Hawaii, following her first lover home. Birch put herself through college there, and then worked her way through law school in California. Corporate life began, first in a five-year stint as a lawyer at San Francisco's prestigious McCutchen, Doyle, Brown & Enersen (presently Bingham McCutchen). By now Birch had become involved in the LGBT community. She had cofounded the south Bay Area's AIDS Legal Services in 1985, and McCutchen was doing a lot of pro bono work, some of which centered on AIDS. "We were all living among the dying and the dead. We were all inundated—it was like living in the Middle Ages during the plague. Everybody needed all of us, all the time. It was one of the finest moments in gay history, because we built all these institutions together, and nursed these young men."

Birch then moved to what was at that time her dream job as a litigator at Apple. "I learned 75 percent of what I know in those years," Birch recalls now. "It was like being in the *Star Wars* bar sometimes. It didn't really matter if you were gay or straight—that was the least of it. It was a revolution, because it was about putting the computer in the hands of the ordinary person. It had a very revolutionary spirit, with complete geniuses living on the very, very edge of what humans know."

After another half a decade, Birch was ready to move on again, and as she fielded offers, the Human Rights Campaign Fund (HRCF) came calling. She was drafted by Hilary Rosen, who was then chairing the HRCF board (Rosen and Birch ended up having a fifteen-year relationship, and share custody of their adopted twins). What she saw on the horizon was Newt Gingrich, and in 1994's midterm elections, the biggest conservative sweep in forty years.

So in 1995, Elizabeth Birch became executive director of the Human Rights Campaign Fund (now the Human Rights Campaign), a move that would not only change her life, but also drastically alter the way this country saw LGBT America. From day one, Birch had a plan, and it was a simple one: "I knew precisely what I would do for the next five years. My goal was to move the discussions out of the streets and into the homes of America. Every piece of communication, every image, every step that we took, we were deliberate, we had a set of goals, and we did not stray from them. Every piece of communication went through a couple of filters: 'If I say these words, will they be heard by the mom in Iowa or the dad in Kentucky?' The other was, 'If a thirteen-year-old LGBT kid hears this, will it affirm them?' I was always looking for a way to move inside the home."

It worked, and HRC began to be not only a gay-household word, but also a major presence in Washington as a lobby for human rights—gay, straight, or otherwise. The drag queen in Tucson, the lesbian in Terre Haute,

Being "The Other"

 LGBT kids are the only people of our species who grow up at the margin of their own nuclear family. Everyone else who's been oppressed, or made to feel like the Other, has at least been able to go home, and everyone looks like them and they feel connected. We grow up in a kind of isolation, which makes the coming out rebirth more powerful."

the tranny teen in Seattle—they all knew who Elizabeth Birch was. And when she came to town to speak, to raise money, to talk about hate crimes, or civil rights, or marriage, she was one of them. Her leadership qualities are vast, her enthusiasm contagious. (Yet she often warned volunteers and staff to keep perspective, that in the scheme of things, this is a tiny movement. Her mantra: "You will never be as famous as Soupy Sales at the bottom of his career.") In many small towns across America, Birch was often the only gay person who had ever sat down to listen. She became a sort of folk hero.

But she was not so folksy that she didn't change HRC's bottom line in a huge way. The budget upon her arrival in January 1995 was $6 million. When she left nine years later, it was nearly $30 million. In that time HRC had also raised $35 million to build a headquarters in the middle of Washington, right there with the big boys.

Birch speaks around the country at colleges, corporations, and other groups about growing up gay, coming out, and diversity. In fact, in her own consulting business, Birch's major focus is on working with corporate clients to take their commitment to diversity much deeper. Was this such a far cry from leading the Human Rights Campaign through nearly a decade of unprecedented growth? Not really. "I come off as very corporate, and that's how I survived," Birch explains. "But the truth is, I'm a capitalist tool with an activist's heart."

And maybe not such a long way from the circus after all.

Ann Bannon

Feckless. *Bildungsroman. Muddled.*

These are not words one hears in everyday conversation. Unless you're speaking to the legendary Ann Bannon.

Now, two more words: Beebo Brinker.

If this is not a familiar name, if you don't know Beebo Brinker, oh, do you have a treat in store for you. Beebo made her first appearance back in 1957, the fever dream of a young wife from Philadelphia, pecking out her first novel on her husband's Remington.

OK, that's a lot to take in. Start over.

Beebo's creator was born Ann Weldy, but to generations of women searching for themselves and other women like them, she is the incomparable Ann Bannon. And for a story where truth is stranger than fiction, Ann Bannon is your girl.

Ann grew up in a suburb of Chicago, and made her way to the University of Illinois in 1950, where she joined a sorority. It was there that Ann started to develop feelings for women that she began to suspect were more than ordinary schoolgirl crushes. "Living in a sorority was like living in a hothouse," she recalls. "I did have feelings, but I never did anything about them." So she did what most young women did at that time. As she put it, "I got my 'Mrs.'" Her husband was older, glamorous, and had traveled the world. Still, she says, "By the time I got married, I hadn't accepted any labels—but I knew I was different."

Different indeed. Shortly after their marriage, Ann hauled out her husband's typewriter one day, put it on their kitchen table, and started writing the lesbian pulp fiction classic, *Odd Girl Out*.

After only one rewrite of her manuscript, Bannon began publishing with Fawcett Gold Medal books, sharing wire-rack spinners with detective novels, westerns, and romances. Her books sold for thirty-five cents each. For anyone who grew up in an era where searching for gay and lesbian fiction was a deep-cover operation, this certainly comes as a shocker. The covers of Bannon's books didn't leave much to the imagination, and what was left out was all there inside. None of this, "And that night, they were not divided"—the single, sort-of-sexy line from Radclyffe Hall's *The Well of Loneliness* that caused it to be banned nearly everywhere. In Bannon's books, men and women partied at Greenwich Village bars, cruised, had sex, even called themselves "gay." Her characters dealt with confusion, shame, newfound joy, and heartache on a very real stage—and any new reader today will find themselves surprised at their

timelessness and authenticity. It seems impossible that Bannon's novels could have been born out of that era—and certainly miraculous that they should have come from this seemingly unlikely source.

Ann's books were resounding successes from the start. In fact, *Odd Girl Out* was Fawcett's second-biggest seller that year. "What we had in the fifties were bars, if you were lucky enough to live in a big city, and the pulps," she notes. These paperbacks sold big because there was no gay and lesbian center, no Internet, no support groups or gay media. And the pulps, it may come as no surprise, also had a huge secondary market: straight men. That the pulps even got through the mail was an incredible feat: The post office, with Congress at its side, continually threatened to withhold delivery of this type of lesbian fiction. They suggested the main character should either commit suicide or suddenly change her mind about her sexuality, and settle down with a man.

But as Bannon's fame grew, her personal life changed little. "At that time, I was starting to be anguished over the choice I had made," she says ruefully, "but in those days it was still pretty scandalous to be gay." But soon the royalty checks were coming in, and before long Ann was making as much as her engineer husband. He loved the extra money, but never asked to see her writing—it was almost like parents who don't want to know their child is gay, though all the signs are there. She had told him the story in *Odd Girl Out* was about "young love and college," and they left it at that.

Publishing Pulp Fiction

 Part of it is that I was writing about women who were coming to terms with a kind of contaminated identity, and every adolescent kid feels it whether they are straight or gay, fat or skinny, black or white. Everybody has that feeling that 'if they really knew how awful I am, I wouldn't have any friends.' So I was writing about something that all young people are going through."

In those years, Ann was visiting New York City's Greenwich Village with newfound friends as often as she could, remaining faithful to her husband and their marriage vows the entire time. It was like field-work: Her eyes were opening up to this brave new world, which she was then recording and passing on for hundreds of thousands of readers to learn from. But the fear of what might happen should she be discovered was nearly unbearable. She remembers going into clubs and asking, "How long since your last raid?" If "two months" was the answer, you moved along until you found a place that was hit just a few nights before. That was as safe as it got. Her memories of what happened if you were caught in a raid in those days those days are still fresh: "Well, they brought out the paddy wagon and they took you down and they booked you and photographed you and the next morning all the New York papers printed the list of the degenerates that had been captured the night before." Here Bannon stops and a cloud crosses her

face. "It would have killed me if that had been me. I don't know what I would have done." She pauses. "But I had to be there."

But a more horrifying incident did take place—one that was more private, but perhaps even harder on her marriage. Ann had been keeping a journal, and the worst possible thing happened: Her husband found it. And read it. "He peeled the bark off me. I thought I was keeping a private diary. I was so ashamed by what he said, and I felt so guilty and so evil. We were living in an apartment with an incinerator shaft and I dropped that thing down the shaft. If I'd had it, I would have had 150 pages of memories that I could use to reconstruct my past. I would give anything to have had the guts to say to him, 'Wait a minute, *that's* part of my life, too.' It might have ended the marriage and it might have been OK. I don't know, but I didn't."

Then, as life would have it, changes came—children, a move to California, and less time each day to drag out the old Remington. Ann Bannon

published six books between 1957 and 1962, and then stopped. She simply never wrote another word. With kids around, and since she was living in a new city, she was lucky to make it to an occasional meeting of the newly formed Daughters of Bilitis meeting. This was the extent of the gay life of the "Queen of Lesbian Pulp Fiction." Bored and dispirited, she went back to school. Did she ever: Eventually, Bannon earned a Ph.D. in linguistics, and became an English professor and dean at Sacramento State.

Before long, of course, word got out on campus: Dr. Weldy was also *Ann Bannon*! One of the male librarians stopped her one day and said, "I just wanted you to know that I just ordered some of your books for the library." She was thrilled. By now it must have seemed like another lifetime—and maybe it was. Perhaps even more touching was an unexpected office visit. She recalls, "One young woman came in with a little bouquet of flowers, which she put on my desk and then said, 'I just found out you are Ann Bannon.'"

Yet she still wasn't out to her family. That changed one night during a party in her home, when a friend from the university was chatting up "Ann's books" with another guest. "What books?" inquired Ann's sixteen-year-old daughter, Inga. Ann notes that suddenly, after years of retirement from the pulp fiction world: "I got shot out of the closet. That was very difficult." After a rough patch with Inga, "she has become my great supporter," and now attends events with her mother all over the country.

Ann Bannon left her husband when all her children finally graduated from college. "I toughed it out: No way were they going to look back and say that I didn't do the right thing," she says now. Ann waited until he was out of town—even then her husband did not want a divorce—"and I packed everything up and moved out."

Today Ann Bannon still has a bit of the college dean air about her . . . but look a little closer, and you'll see the spark that dreamed up "that swashbuckling, six-foot butch Beebo Brinker" more than fifty years ago. Her awards now spill over the small table she initially set aside for them, and a play she wrote called *The Beebo Brinker Chronicles* has run in several cities across the nation. She even had a cup of coffee with her ex-husband a couple of years ago, who grudgingly told her he'd recently read *Odd Girl Out*. "It wasn't half-bad," he admitted.

Ann Bannon's books were "love letters to women I thought I'd never meet," she admits. Love letters that became literary saviors, and an avenue to freedom for women everywhere.

Lisa Sherman

That Lisa Sherman is just like her grandmother, one of her own greatest heroines, seems like an obvious comparison. "She was an extraordinary person," recalls Sherman. "I think the definition of a hero is someone who has the courage to do the right thing. My grandmother was just a rock. She got her entire family out of Russia to the United States in 1909. She found a way, as the oldest of eight kids, to be the mother and the sister." Betty Sherman was a leader, a protector, someone who did the right thing at any cost, enlightening and fighting for her own.

Lisa has become very much like Betty, though her "family" is much larger, and spread out all across the country. If you haven't heard of Lisa Sherman, you've certainly heard of her employer: Viacom's MTV Networks. She is executive vice president and general manager of Logo, the all-gay-all-the-time television channel. Sherman laughingly calls herself "a professional gay person," but it's true. And the story of her coming into this wry moniker is a particularly arduous one.

Lisa's life growing up was never a hardship like her grandmother's—it was as American as, in her case, football. The older of two daughters growing up in Philadelphia, she seems to have been born a Philadelphia Eagle, with a huge extended family to round out the team. "We were like the Jewish Kennedys. There wasn't a Thanksgiving my whole life growing up, no matter where we were in the country, all my cousins, my sister and I, would do whatever we could to get back to Philly to play in our family football games."

She describes herself as the classic first child. "You take on a responsibility and a seriousness," Sherman insists. "There's a push to be successful at whatever it is you do—and please your parents. I didn't disappoint. I was a decent athlete; I'd make varsity, and my dad would say, 'When are you going to be captain?' I always managed to get myself into leadership positions, and found myself creating teams of people and getting us all thinking about how to do something together."

But by the time Sherman was a senior in college, she was still unsure of her future, and had run into a major snag in the parent-pleasing department: She had discovered she was a lesbian. "I had a really close friend, and I asked her if she wanted to live with a few of us in the dorm, and—I remember it vividly—we were in my room, and she said, 'I don't think I can.' I asked why, and she said, 'Because I'm gay, and I have a girlfriend.' And the minute she said that, I thought, 'Holy shit, I think I'm gay.' The light just went on." She eventually became Lisa's first girlfriend. "But I didn't come out to anybody. It became a big secret that the two of us kept. I was terribly ashamed. I was freaked out. The kid who always did everything their parents wanted them to do. I could not imagine how I was going to live my life like this."

Knowing she had a head for business, Lisa opted for a training program after college at the telecom firm that was at that time called Bell Atlantic. She enjoyed a long and mostly happy career at the company; had worked there sixteen years and was a senior vice president when she was required to attend a diversity seminar. It was 1993. She was not out at work. This would be a day that changed her life.

Even now, all these years later, Lisa's voice tightens when she tells the story of that day.

"So for the very first exercise, the facilitator put these easels all around the room, and at the top of each one was a group, so it would say: WOMEN ARE, MEN ARE, BLACKS ARE, LATINOS ARE, JEWS ARE, GAYS ARE. . . . What was ridiculous about it was that he wanted you to go up and write the first candid thing you thought.

How Lisa Sherman Brought Authenticity Home

The day I left Bell Atlantic, I told my boss, 'It took two years just to get the two words *sexual orientation* written into the diversity policy. If you want people to be their most creative, their most innovative, then they have to be able to bring their whole selves to work. There's a guy who I work with, and his partner died of AIDS, and he couldn't tell anybody. So he had to come to work every day and act like nothing had happened. So how does he deal with his grief and be here 100 percent working for you?'"

Everyone could see what you were writing. It was ridiculous. So things were pretty benign. JEWS LIKE BIG OFFICES. That was mine. Then you get to GAYS ARE, and obviously, no one knew there were gay people in the room. I was literally sick. I thought my head was going to explode. All the things that were written about gays were bad. GAYS ARE PERVERTED, GAYS SPREAD DISEASE, GAYS WILL TRY AND CONVERT MY CHILDREN—I mean, it was just horrific.

"I came out of that room, threw up, and went back to my office. I swore to myself that day that I was going to leave the company, and that the day that I left I was going to go see the president of the company, Ray Smith. I was going to stay in the closet and find a new job, and then leave.

"It took two years. But during those two years I was becoming more resentful and more angry. When I would see people who were in that diversity seminar in meetings, I could never look at them the same way. So the last day at Bell Atlantic I went up to see Ray Smith, who I had known for years. He thought I was just coming to say good-bye—and so he was very warm, and invited me into his office and I said, 'Well, Ray, I've been here for eighteen years and there's something you don't know about me, and that is that I'm gay.' He didn't act surprised, but I knew he was shocked. I told him that I wanted him to know that one of the reasons I was leaving was that I didn't feel comfortable there. And though it wouldn't affect me, I wanted him to know because I was hoping that he could help other people who would still be there. I told him about the diversity meeting; I told him that I never felt safe coming out there; I told him there was a group below him who were blocking policies. That was the kind of candid conversation we had. And he got it."

Indeed he did. A month later Ray Smith appeared at a meeting on domestic partnership at Bell Atlantic and said, "On her last day here, Lisa Sherman came to my office and came out. She told me this policy was being blocked. And I didn't believe her. But I've sat and listened here for the last hour, and I'm horrified to see that she was right." Smith began to help change the company policy then and there.

So, a few years later, when Lisa Sherman worried that she had no network experience as she interviewed at the fledgling Logo channel, her business acumen and years of activism in the LGBT community—much of it with the Human Rights Campaign—quickly convinced boss Brian Graden that she was made for the job. Lisa remembers, "In my interview, he asked as a last, offbeat question, 'What's your biggest fear?' I thought for a minute and said, 'Getting it right, because so many people will be counting on

us to do that.' He looked at me and got all teary-eyed and said, 'That's my biggest fear, too.' So this match made in heaven struck a deal, and at this writing, the little company that started in 2005 with a handful of employees and three advertisers is in fifty million homes, with more than 200 advertisers.

Lisa loves talking about Logo—it's clear she loves her job. "I want people to know that Logo is really about telling authentic stories," Sherman says (who surely knows from authentic stories). "I feel like we've created an amazing culture—it feels very mission-driven. It feels like there's a higher purpose to what we're doing."

Lisa Sherman's friends call her the ultimate Girl Scout. To speak with her, hear her enthusiasm when she talks about Logo, or football, or her friends and family, you might instead think head cheerleader. Certainly one gets the feeling that doing the right thing—just like Betty Sherman did for *her* family always comes first. "My grandmother used to tell me that the only reward for doing good work is getting more work." If that's true, Lisa Sherman's going to be busy for a very long time.

Roberta Achtenberg

There's a twisted, flower-and-tree-covered walk up to Roberta Achtenberg's hidden house at the top of Noe Valley, and it's a stairway to heaven. If you were to embed yourself in a cause, a project, a battle—like Achtenberg does—this is where you would go to fight it out, and then restore yourself. It's a little like one imagines it would be walking up the steps to Armistead Maupin's 28 Barbary Lane from *Tales of the City*, but with one of our greatest LGBT activists at the end of the climb, instead of treachery and gay mayhem.

Roberta Achtenberg is a California girl, born and bred; a kid from Inglewood and the daughter of immigrants. Her father came to the United States from Russia, her mother from Quebec; they met and married in a Jewish immigrant neighborhood in Los Angeles and ran a grocery store there. Like so many new citizens, they were interested in social justice and the politics of their adopted country, and passed that on to their children. "My parents were very hardworking and very honest people. We talked politics all

the time. Some people are red diaper babies. My father was very anti-communist because that's what he fled when he left Soviet Russia. Jews didn't fare particularly well in either the Tsar's army or the Soviet army."

Dinner-table politics evidently made their mark on a very young Roberta Achtenberg. Her very first political act took place outside a restaurant when she was only seven years old. Workers were demonstrating on the sidewalk, and at a time when other little girls were simply refusing to eat their broccoli, Roberta was refusing to eat somewhere there were alleged unfair labor practices. Achtenberg says simply, "I just knew that we shouldn't cross that picket line." And this is how the life of an activist begins.

Roberta's growing interest in social justice continued as she came of age in the 1960s when she graduated from college at the University of California at Berkeley. Those were heady days. She married, and continued on to law school, transferring to the University of Utah, where her new husband had received a fellowship. When his time there was finished, he returned to San Francisco, and Roberta stayed on to finish her degree. "That's when I met my first lesbian lover," Achtenberg recalls. "My husband and I then struggled for two or three years to see if we could find a way to figure this out. But it was not really meant to be. In the interim, my brother died and then my mother died, so those were tough years. Certainly they were complicated years. It was

a struggle, but I know people who've put themselves through that struggle for ten or more years. Now that's tough. Comparatively, I was able to reorganize my life in fairly short order and get on with living the life I was meant to live. I feel very grateful for that."

Though history often rises out of the need for change, perhaps just as often a true activist is born out of that change. "Certainly where and when you live matter significantly," Achtenberg continues. "Had it not been for the civil rights movement, the women's rights movement, all the opportunity that I had, to imagine myself as a lawyer and then to become a lawyer, and then to get hired to do the things that I was hired to do, and then to be able to make a living at doing work that I cared about and believed in—they are all gifts. There is no virtue that I possess necessarily that made all of that happen."

So Achtenberg set out to make a change, first from the inside, teaching law, and then by serving as dean at the New College of California Law School. Then, in 1977, she joined Donna Hitchens to work the grassroots angle: They started the Lesbian Rights Project, which has blossomed into the National Center for Lesbian Rights.

"It was much more modest in the early days," Achtenberg points out, "simply because our worldview was much more constricted. Lesbian groups were not created to address political issues: They did family law. What was thought of as political was sodomy law and employment law. Helping women keep custody of their children was thought of as an exclusively lesbian issue. Our first publication was *The Guide to Lesbian Mother Custody*. Domestic partners—we called them family partners—second-parent adoption, they were thought of at the time as 'girl's stuff.' There was no broad-based adherence to 'the personal is political.' We've come to that in this movement only more recently."

The political really did become personal for Achtenberg soon enough. Though she ran unsuccessfully for the California State Assembly in 1988, she won the race for San Francisco Board of Supervisors just two years later. "To be an elected official; to be an appointed official and to do the community development work that I do now, these are all extraordinary privileges," she says emotionally.

But Roberta Achtenberg's most famous political position was a fight for the ages. The LGBT community saw one of their own get called up at last by newly elected President Clinton, when he tapped Achtenberg in 1993 to be Assistant Secretary of Housing and Urban Development (HUD) for Fair Housing and Equal Opportunity. This would be the first time ever that a gay appointee would need Senate confirmation, and North Carolina's uber-conservative Senator Jesse Helms was determined to stop Roberta in her tracks. "That damn lesbian" is what the world remembers Helms calling Achtenberg. But it went much further than that.

"Everybody was taken aback, really," admits Achtenberg. "We thought we knew what it would be like, but we didn't really. Some people said, 'It was so brave of you.' Naiveté can be a great thing. If we had known at the outset what it might be like, I certainly would have hesitated. But you don't know and then, hey, I've jumped off the cliff; I'm in this to win now.

Being Able to Serve, and Serve with Distinction

 My job in lesbian and gay history was to have been the first [LGBT person to pass Senate confirmation] and to have won, which I understand and accept and am proud about. But I didn't do it to do it, I did it to serve. I will tell you this: I don't know that I've ever gotten used to being called every name in the book and having my honesty and integrity questioned, because you never really get used to that, but when they attacked my child, well, that I will never abide."

You are not on the Senate floor participating, you're reading about all of this in the paper."

Meanwhile, Helms was on the Senate floor, wreaking havoc: "She's not your garden-variety lesbian," he raged. "She's a militant, activist, mean lesbian, working her whole career to advance the homosexual agenda. I'm not going to put a lesbian in a position like that. If you want to call me a bigot, fine."

The rest of the Senate ostensibly did call him a bigot, and Helms lost that battle, sending a determined Achtenberg on to serve HUD and the Clinton administration brilliantly. Yet San Francisco had a grip on her. She returned to run for mayor in 1995, losing the race by an unexpectedly narrow margin. Except for a brief return to Washington, D.C., as a senior adviser at HUD, and a more recent stint leading a HUD transition team before President Obama took office, Roberta has been back in her San Francisco aerie. "I was happy to do it for a discrete period of time, and then happy to come home" is Achtenberg's take on her last Washington gig. And there's that word again. Housing. Home. Currently, as a Workforce and Economic Development consultant, she is advising a company that is one of the country's largest home-builders, developing San Francisco's Hunter's Point Shipyard and Candlestick Point.

But wherever it is, whatever she does, the politician, activist, and mother who says she's "optimistic, lighthearted, and cries at the drop of a hat" will likely be waiting outside some virtual—or perhaps real—restaurant door, putting up the good fight. You can count on it.

Rep. Tammy Baldwin

An odd thing about being a member of Congress: You spend a good part of your career standing up for people you don't often see, people who are living in a place you love so much that you've got to move away to protect it. Congressman Barney Frank, for example, spends a lot of his time in Washington, D.C., looking out for the rights of New Bedford, Massachusetts, fisherman—an unlikely group of Frank supporters, you may think, but they adore him. Though Frank outed himself in the halls of Congress in 1987, his compatriot—the only other out member of Congress—has run as a gay person "from scratch," as she calls it, all the way back since her first race in 1986 for county supervisor. Her name is Tammy Baldwin.

Tammy Baldwin loves her hometown. In fact, except for her years at Smith College (yes, more on that later), she has resided in Madison, Wisconsin, all her life. She and her partner, Lauren Azar, live in an old house in town, which they restored themselves. (When asked if doing home improvements was really the way she wanted to spend her one day off a week, she gives a wry smile, shrugs, and says, "Well, it is together time. . . .") Since being elected to Congress in 1998, she spends a lot of time in Washington. She is exactly

the sort of legislator a voter wants: She is as likely to be in touch with the problems of guy who owns the hardware store as she is with the views of a senator from the other side of the country.

As a little girl, Tammy lived with her maternal grandparents who had given their young, now-divorced daughter the chance to go back to college and earn her degree. She was always present in her daughter's life, but Tammy learned much at the hands of her scientist grandfather and costume designer grandmother—a fascinating left/right brain couple whom she adored. It all made for an interesting learning experience, especially when it came to politics.

"If I think of childhood experiences," Baldwin says, "I think of my grandparents, who interacted with democracy in very traditional ways: They voted and wrote to their elected officials. My mother, when she returned to campus to get her degree, became a hippie, a Vietnam War protestor, and was very active in the anti-segregation movement. I saw her as an activist in the street and my grandparents as much more traditional. But both were examples for me of watching adults make change happen by playing active roles. By the time I was midway through middle school, I thought that even I could make some of those differences."

Before she could start making the Big Difference in Washington, Tammy made her mark at Smith College. Smith is one of the few remaining women's colleges, and an institution that has long had a high feminist—and in the last generation or so, lesbian—profile.

(The year 1975 saw a flurry of Smith College T-shirts sporting the slogan "A Century of Women on Top.") So it's not much of a surprise that Baldwin met her first girlfriend here.

"It was a supportive environment for the time, which was 1982. Most women's colleges were struggling with not wanting the image of being bastions of lesbianism, but I felt such great support from my straight classmates. It was a very positive place to come out.

"What I remember is the consciousness-raising sessions in the house system, where you could invite groups to discuss racism, sexism, or homophobia. I have a vivid memory of our house always welcoming these discussions, but when there was a session on homophobia, some of the more close-minded classmates said things like we needed to draw some lines or else next we'll be supporting murderers or something equally heinous. I remember thinking, 'Wait just a minute!' It was the first time I'd heard anyone equate gays and lesbians with criminals." Though she admits this was an isolated incident, she still recalls, "I reeled from having LGBT issues cast in such stark terms."

It was an injustice that stuck with her. By 1986, she was running her first political race. "The Dane County Board of Supervisors seat was the only position I held where I wasn't the first openly gay politician to run," Baldwin recalls. "I was the first openly gay or lesbian candidate when I ran for state legislature. In Congress there were other gays or lesbians who had come out before, but they had been

outed or came out during their term of office. Before that, the LGBT community just didn't think it could be done, electing somebody who was out. Prior to my election, the only way that was done was by locking someone in the closet, electing them to office, and then reelecting them as out people."

Equally important to her is that she was the first woman from Wisconsin to be elected to Congress. "It shattered a glass ceiling. Little girls can look up and see somebody that looks like them sitting in an office and say, 'I can do anything. I can do *this*.'"

What it comes down to is that Baldwin is stalwart. Stalwart, dedicated, and single-minded in the very best way. She has her eye on the prize and will not be deterred. And for anyone who doubts this, look at the issues she cared about when she first ran for county supervisor: LGBT rights and health care reform. Meet her for five minutes and you know that these are things she still cares about, and that she will not stop until she reaches her goal.

"The two issues that I'm probably most known for are the need for universal health care and LGTB equality. It should also be noted that I came into politics in the middle of the AIDS epidemic in the Midwest. While it was already widely known about on both coasts, our first cases in Wisconsin were cases of people who were probably diagnosed on one of the coasts and decided to come back home to die."

But what is it like to come to Capitol Hill as an outsider? And to have one of your major life and political quests be such an unpopular one? "Certainly there are detractors," she admits, "predominately from home, not when I'm here in Washington. I do get some hate mail, but that's usually more associated with votes that I'm casting as opposed to attacking me as a person. But there is some of that, too.

"Here in Washington, my colleagues are politicians and have learned how to get along with people they may disagree with, and I find that, with very few exceptions, there is a civility and friendliness in most cases. What I feel most often is the hypocrisy of someone who actually might like me yet goes to the floor and casts a vote against LGBT equality. They feel like they have to and I get the confessions of, 'I really wish I didn't have to do this.' And I keep saying, 'Well, you don't!'"

To that end, she and Barney Frank have begun the LGBT Equality Caucus in the halls of Congress, with great success. "When I first started serving in Congress, we were fighting a lot of defensive battles: Anti-gay amendments and legislation were frequently being brought to the floor. Republicans were using God, guns, and gays to drive wedges. There was no structure to prepare us to defend against these bills and amendments. But there were people helping, and they were working hard. I thought, 'some of these people would like to get credit in their home districts for being strong allies and stepping up to the plate, so why don't we call it something and give titles if they're really hard worker bees, and let others just

Our Bright Future?

 I think that on a national level over the next ten years we will have come close to achieving full legal equality. I do think that after we pass the first civil rights law impacting the LGTB community, ENDA (Employment Non-Discrimination Act), that that will be a bright light. We will have said that discrimination exists, it's wrong, and now it's illegal. Once you say that, just as with the passage of the Civil Rights Act of the sixties, it becomes wrong to discriminate in housing, public accommodations, education, etc. Once you've establish that this discrimination is wrong, there's nothing for such discrimination to rest upon in these other arenas."

affiliate if they want to get credit back home and issue a press release.' It turned out to be quite wonderful. This really is the core group that works on our issues and makes sure that we're ready for these debates. I was thrilled to see how many of my colleagues put out press releases and got stories in gay and straight papers back home." Baldwin gives a little laugh of surprise. "We founded it in June 2008 and we have more than eighty members now. At the inaugural meeting we had something like twenty vice chairs."

Tammy Baldwin seems to thrive on a combination of hope and drive. When asked if there has been a single moment that changed her life forever, her answer is clear and swift: "The election of Barack Obama." But before she can extrapolate, a buzzer and announcement interrupt. It's then one realizes she seems to have one ear cocked at all times. Today it's a call to the floor for a vote in fifteen minutes. She brightens visibly. This is what Tammy Baldwin lives for.

Lisa Vogel

"I hadn't ever produced anything but a good kegger."

And why would she have? Lisa Vogel was only nineteen years old when she started her first real job. And she's still at that same job today. Vogel is the brains—and the brawn—behind the Michigan Womyn's Music Festival, the famed weeklong cultural experience that's been a lesbian summer destination location since 1976.

There aren't many folks these days who have had the same job their whole life. That's a pre–baby boomer way of life, where your dad worked for the insurance company his whole life, and your mom was a nurse. It was the steady thing to do: You put in your time, hung it up when you turned sixty-five, and got your pension. But "Michigan" or "the Festival," as it's often simply called, isn't a job for Vogel, it's truly a vocation.

Lisa was what they would have called a go-getter back in the late sixties when she was a little kid. "I was kind of entrepreneurial. I had all these little jobs I made up for myself; I had a skateboard business—I made skateboards for other kids. I would buy the discount candy at the mill for 3 cents and sell it for 5 cents. I was really good at marbles, so I would win marbles, and I would trade marbles with these kids whose dad sold comic books. I made rubber guns—I was a little baby dyke—then I'd make a promotional six-foot rubber gun and sell the pistols, so I was constantly doing things like that. We were kind of poor, so we all worked really young. Cleaning up other people's yards, shoveling snow. By the time I was sixteen, I worked full-time—and I was also a drug dealer."

Ba-boom! How to drop a bomb into the conversation. "I sold pot and mescaline and LSD and things like that," she says, ticking them off, one by one, on her fingers. "I was a senior in high school and I had my own apartment, which was my drug-selling situation. I was sort of precocious. I didn't move out from home—I just 'stayed with friends' a lot."

So while all the other girls were at cheerleading tryouts, Vogel was leading the bad girl life. C'mon, imagine having your own *crib* at sixteen? Her parents were in the dark about her sideline (and the bachelorette pad). "I was a little hippie in high school—going to a lot of rock shows and concerts."

Lisa set off for college at Central Michigan University in Mount Pleasant, always listening to as much music as she could. She thinks of herself, even today, as very much a child of the seventies, or as she puts it, "definitely part of the countercultural youth. It very much informs my work still. Because the values of that time were something I took seriously. I took the drugs seriously, I took the partying seriously, I went to a rock show a couple of times a week. I was very much into the rock-and-roll scene."

"The music was happy then," she muses. "And the music was angry, and there was a lot of hope. There was determination that we could make a difference. And our value system meant something, which sort of segues into the feminist and lesbian-feminist movement." And then came the weekend that was her own personal segue. One particular invitation to a weekend away—with *no* music—got her entrepreneurial soul going.

"I was starting sophomore year, and one of the professors was trying to pick me up. She was straight and exploring her lesbianism and she invited me to go to Missouri to this women's festival. Away we went. A couple hundred women: workshops, communal living—not music—shared food, howling at the moon. I had never been to anything like it." Vogel laughs. "I was totally mesmerized by the process and the possibility: I went to millions of festivals, but the idea that I could go to one that was just for women was completely new."

Vogel was hooked. "So soon after that, a bunch of us got in a van and we drove out to a women's festival in Boston, and we heard all this music, and a lot of the artists I know and love were there. So we went every day and had to leave every night, all stoned in the van, and I said, 'Wouldn't it be great if we didn't have to leave every night? We could all just be together.' Nobody was really biting. I just kept talking to people, and eventually someone from the Mount Pleasant community, Mary Kindig, said, 'Yeah, we could probably do that.' So she and my sister and I produced that first Michigan Womyn's Music Festival.

"I was in college; I had no money. I was no longer a drug dealer, but I borrowed money from my drug dealer and bought postage stamps. We had rummage sales, even a car wash once—pathetic fund-raisers!—and we'd break into the college offices and run off some flyers. We went away to a music festival in Champagne, and the people were saying, 'Oh no, you cannot be promoting this big music festival with this *thing*.' We didn't have anything else to hand out except hundreds of these flyers. But I had a cooler full of beer, so anybody who said they would bring a hundred flyers back to their home community, I would give a cold beer. And it worked."

It worked all right. Two thousand women showed up at the first Michigan Womyn's Music Festival. They hoped they might get a couple of hundred. "We didn't know what we were doing," Vogel admits now. "The most amazing thing was to choose to do the second year, because the first was so terrorizing." Stories she tells sound like the lesbian Keystone Kops: the food co-op folks she hired to serve up the three daily vegetarian meals who went out for a swim the first day and never returned; trying to set up the stage and running back to put out a fire in the field; trying to get someone to take away the garbage bags now exploding in the sun; and their paltry $400 profit. Who would do this a second time?

Lisa Vogel would, and she's done it every year since, and for the same reasons as when she started. She's clean and sober now, but her beliefs are the same. And many women come back again and again who feel the same as Vogel. Some years as many as 7,000 participate—and now, a good number of them are straight women. Of course it's about the music, the programs, and the workshops, but women will

The Price of Listening

 We are from a population where people often think, 'There's nobody listening to us.' I really endeavor to listen to the minority, and to the tone. I personally read every feedback sheet we get from the Festival and I have for thirty-five years. It keeps it real for me. Every once in a while I go, 'Wow, ow, that really fucking hurts.' And other times, I'll have tears running down my face. Otherwise, I should just go do a music show."

tell you Festival is bigger than the sum of its parts. They understand the draw of the counterculture, and wait all year to come back and camp out in a tent and share it with the people and the land they consider home.

"Festival pushes me all the time to walk the talk," Lisa says seriously. "What women write to us all the time is that it gives them the strength to go on and be more of who they are. There's a culture at Festival that's very tangible. If you talk to people who go there, that's what they experience: 'Michigan culture.' People refer to it in different ways. OK, I came out in the seventies, but one of the things that was different was that we actively moved away from materialism. Getting the *things* was not what was important. Saving the planet? We were just starting to not litter! We weren't even recycling. We were thinking about stopping a war; we were thinking about liberating our bodies—women as well as men. We were thinking making money was not the most important thing. The most important thing was to make a difference. The most important thing was to be an agent of change. We didn't have that language then—but that's what we meant."

It's strong stuff, and every year Lisa Vogel leaves her lovely Berkeley, California, home to go to rural Michigan, live in a tent for nearly six weeks, and experience it all over again. It takes a village, and each August Vogel and her staff (plus Festival goers, who all volunteer for eight hours during their stay) put one together on the 650 acres they now own.

But really, after doing the job since 1976, one wonders: Does Vogel ever think of quitting? "I want Festival to stay in place long enough for the wind beneath the wings of feminism to get stronger again. And I see it in the younger women. Listen, I went through the eighties and nineties. I got complacent. I wanted "My Things." I cared more about a vacation than something else; I think we all took a hit during Reaganomics. We all drank the Kool-Aid in one way or another. But we're once again in a place of reexamining our values. That shift has started."

Funny thing. When asked what she might have done if she hadn't brainstormed the Festival she replies: "I used to think back in the seventies that I was going to be a women's studies professor."

Hell, what does Lisa Vogel think she's been *doing* all these years?

Urvashi Vaid

"I am a geek."

While speaking to Urvashi Vaid, she says this more than once, but nothing could be further from the truth. What she *is* is thoughtful, fascinating, and inspiring, of course.

Having a conversation with Urvashi is like being given a shiny, new primer in racism, feminism, activism, and social justice, all rolled into one. And not one of those *Introduction to . . .* textbooks you get freshman year of college, either. This is more like the *Insider's Guide* that's full of critical information and wonderful anecdotes, written in an accessible style, with a dash of self-deprecating good humor. Urvashi Vaid makes it sound

so easy—but pay close attention. It's not.

Urvashi was born in New Delhi, India, and moved to the small college town of Potsdam, New York, with her family at the age of eight. (Snow! She'd never seen any before.) Her parents were both the first in their families to go to college, and her father excelled, receiving a Fulbright Scholarship to work on his Ph.D. in the United States. "Their decision to relocate to the U.S. was the same as it was for most immigrants," recalls Urvashi. "Better opportunities for them, and getting their children a better education." So the mid-sixties brought the Vaids and their three daughters to upstate New York, where they were pleased and surprised to find an active Indian community. Urvashi, being a bit younger than her sisters, was excited about the move. To her, an adventure was about to begin.

The LGBT myth about Urvashi was that she became an activist by the age of eleven, though she scoffs at this. "I think that is an inflated way of saying it. I was politically aware, as a result of growing up in the sixties in a college town. There were demonstrations in the street about the Vietnam War, I had older siblings who were tuned in a little more, and I had parents who encouraged me to read the paper and watch the news. Dinner-table talk was always about current events or books. So there was always encouragement to pay attention. And I was always interested, although I couldn't tell you why. From an early age, I was always tuned in to politics." Tuned in indeed. "The first political letter that I wrote was written around 1968 or 1969 and addressed to Richard M. Nixon, urging him to sign the antiballistic missile treaty," she admits. "What a nerd!"

Urvashi had an advantage most kids never experience, though: a global perspective that set her off early on the trail toward social justice. "I think being an immigrant definitely shapes my worldview because I had a bicultural or multicultural world consciousness. We spoke Hindi and Punjabi, ate Indian food, and we were very Indian-identified, but here we were in America with American friends and a whole different set of traditions and things to learn. So, we had a whole set of experiences to learn while simultaneously living in multiple worlds. I also think that the experience of being an immigrant gave me a view of poverty and inequality in a very visceral way that was a formative experience of my life. Back then, India was this exotic land from far, far away—and it was all about mysticism. Kids in my class would ask me if I lived in a teepee; they were confused about the kind of Indian that I was."

By the time Urvashi started college at Vassar, her views of politics, society, and gender discrimination were perhaps more sophisticated than those of most students. She came out strong as a feminist before she declared herself a lesbian. "My first experience organizing was producing conferences and women's cultural stuff, and through those kinds of experiences I got exposed to meeting lesbians and I began to think, 'Well, gee, am I one?' I didn't know what I was. Then

What Makes Me Fight

 I think visually watching the footage in the sixties and seeing marchers being water-cannoned with dogs attacking and the brutality of the police at the time against the anti-war protestors; that had a big influence on me. Coming up in the gay rights movement, I participated in and organized a number of protests: violence against women; police violence against gay people; police raids on gay bars; the lack of response on violence against gay people; all issues where the government was not taking seriously the rights of all the people or worse, those cases where the government was sponsoring or condoning the violence against us through these really violent and brutal acts."

I fell into bed with women as well as with men. What can I say? I was nineteen and twenty, and active. First I thought I was bisexual, but as it came together for me physically and emotionally, I realized that I was a lesbian."

Graduation saw her organizing spark take hold. Urvashi moved to Boston, aware that there was a strong activist community, and began to immerse herself in the LGBT movement in earnest. She began volunteering at the *Gay Community News* and got her law degree from Northeastern University ("in my spare time," she says, without a trace of irony), and started the Boston Lesbian/Gay Political Alliance, an organization to help the gay community increase their involvement in the political process.

It seemed inevitable that Urvashi should turn to Washington, and she ended up there next, working on the National Prison Project for the American Civil Liberties Union. "I loved public-interest law—federal civil rights lawsuits—but I was really doing all of this activism on the side and was getting more and more into it." It was during this time that Urvashi first became involved with the National Gay and Lesbian Task Force (NGLTF) as a member of their board of directors. By now she knew she wanted a job deep in the community, and in 1989, she became the task force's media director, determined to make the LGBT movement part of mainstream news. "We had some pretty big successes," she admits. "The march on Washington in 1987 helped to build an infrastructure

within the movement, because people went home and started a lot of local organizations; the 1993 march helped politicize the gay movement, and people were much more politically aware after that march."

But Urvashi Vaid yearned to have her own say, and, taking a hiatus, moved to Provincetown, Massachusetts, to work on her seminal 1995 book, *Virtual Equality*, which won the Stonewall Book Award. "Gay people do not fight for freedom to live in a lavender bubble, but in a more just society" is an oft-quoted line from Vaid's book. So, book in hand, Urvashi returned to Washington and NGLTF, where she served as executive director until her departure for the Ford Foundation. No one was more surprised to find herself there than Urvashi.

"I told [the headhunter who called me] that I was too radical to work for a place like the Ford Foundation and she said, 'No, just go talk to this guy.' I did and loved the guy. He had all of this international experience, and I thought that I could really learn from these people. I did; Ford was like graduate school with money. They sent me to graduate school to study social change organizing and paid me to do it."

From 2005 to mid-2010, Urvashi served as executive director of the Arcus Foundation, a chance to see LGBT issues as part of the social justice framework, "which speaks to me and my whole life." Aside from funding community projects, Arcus also worked to ensure conservation of the great apes.

Urvashi has begun work on her second book, but she's still everywhere: Turn around and you'll spy her at any number of events, often turned out in a stunning jewel-colored sari, likely as not beside her longtime girlfriend, comedian Kate Clinton. She's certainly no stranger to awards and accolades: Before she was forty, *Time* magazine heralded her as one of the "Fifty for the Future"; *The Advocate* has named her Woman of the Year; and *Out* named her one of the fifty most influential people in America in 2009.

But listening to Urvashi Vaid, you know her fight is far from over. This is the woman who held up a sign in 1990 at President Bush's first policy speech on AIDS that read TALK IS CHEAP; AIDS FUNDING IS NOT. (She was led away by the police.)

Urvashi Vaid is nothing if not a force of nature, and she's still got plenty on her mind: "I guess what I am trying to say is that whether it is it assimilation or integration, being gay gives us the opportunity to reinvent and reimagine ways of being. We do gender in different ways; we have family and friendships in slightly different ways than our parents did; we have experienced being outsiders, being shunned, labeled deviant and demonized, called sinners and bad people; and out of all those experiences our challenge is to create a society with a policy and in a world that doesn't include those exclusions."

Rabbi Sharon Kleinbaum

Just for starters: How many rabbis do you know who have been in prison with Charles Manson's girls?

Sure, that's sort of a shocker of a way to introduce one of *Time* magazine's "Top 50 Rabbis" (#17 in 2008), but it certainly does say it all about Rabbi Sharon Kleinbaum. She is an anomaly: a Jewish scholar with a wicked sense of humor, whose life's mission is to find a way to mix religion, social justice, and sexuality. Oh, and she's a lesbian. And really young looking, too. Kleinbaum laughs, "This is just about the only career choice where it's really not great to look this young."

Rabbi Kleinbaum is at once easygoing and very serious. It's a combination that has drawn countless allies and congregants into her camp. That camp is Greenwich Village's Congregation Beth Simchat Torah, or as everyone calls it, CBST. It is the largest LGBT synagogue in the world.

Even as a teenager, Sharon was following her own private path, wrapping herself in both the comforts and complexities of her religion. When the public school system in her hometown of Rutherford, New Jersey, started

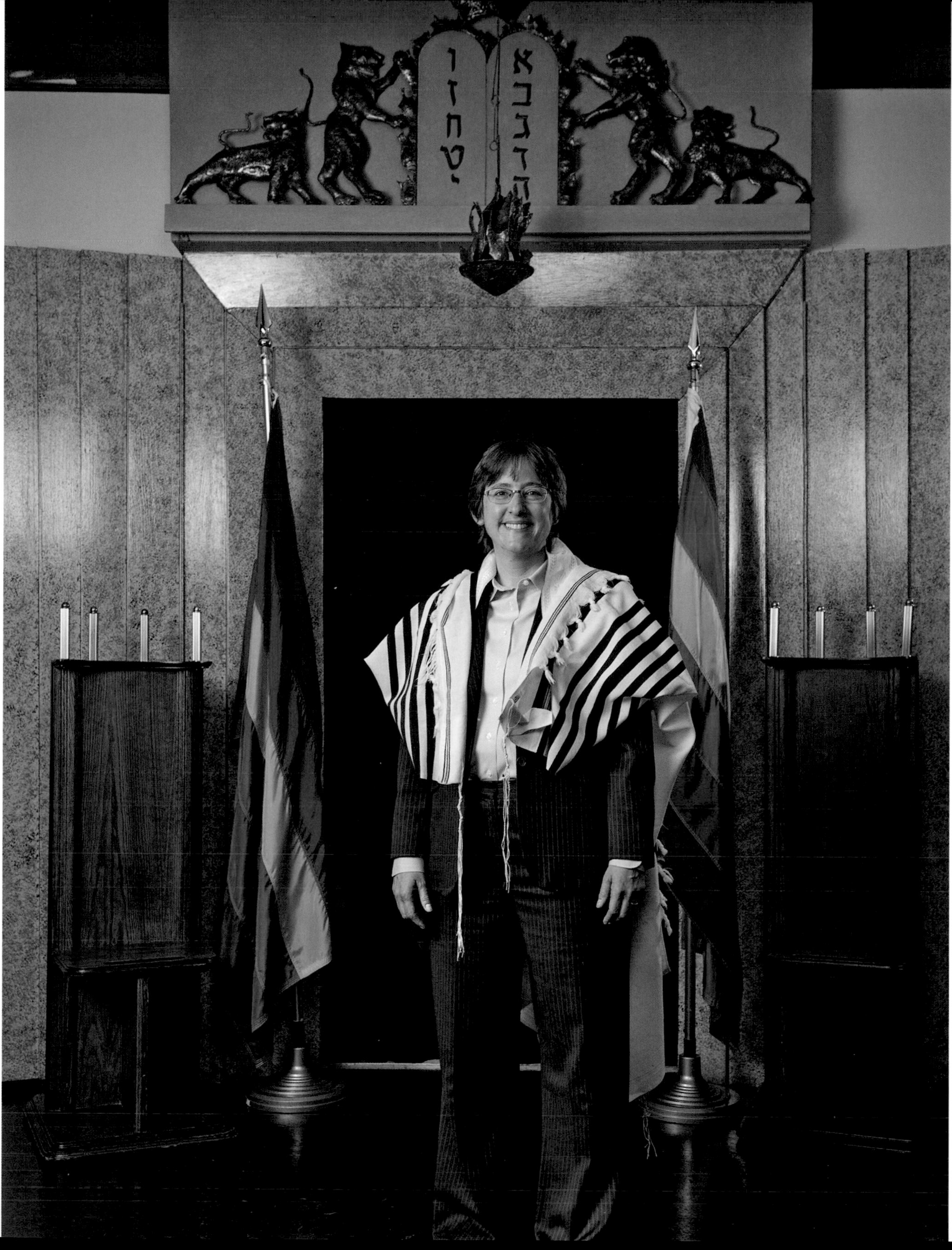

א ב ג ד ה
ו ז ח ט י

to crumble, she told her parents she wanted to attend an Orthodox Jewish high school. "I definitely became more Orthodox than they were comfortable with, but from their perspective it was better than other things I could have done. So for me it was a really profound time of learning and being surrounded by adults who actually cared about big questions, and it was, intellectually, extremely stimulating and exciting. It was a place where I was treated by the adults as a young adult, not as a child. I loved it."

But by the time college neared, Sharon's feelings had begun to change. "I started leaving Orthodoxy. I no longer could feel comfortable with the Orthodox attitude toward women. It was very painful—it was a whole other kind of coming out. Retrospectively, I can imagine there were gay issues for me that were beneath the surface." Basically, she explains, "It no longer felt like home."

Kleinbaum had, in fact, started to consider that she might be a lesbian; she even snuck off to the local college library, away from prying small-town eyes, to research the subject of homosexuality. "I was confused. I had no idea what was going on. I just kept waiting for a switch to turn, and all the feelings I had about girls would go toward boys; I just thought I was in a developmental thing. The switch apparently never happened." An early relationship with a woman at Barnard College involved much skullduggery and fear, and Kleinbaum believes that much of that fear and shame is as prevalent today as it was for her in

the late seventies. She sees it today at CSBT. "It is intense the amount of shame and anxiety and pain people go through to come out and to not kill themselves. The straight world doesn't get it. For most of my congregants, coming to services on Friday night for an hour and a half is the only time they live in a majority culture."

The mantle Rabbi Kleinbaum adopted when she was hired by CBST in 1992 was a heavy one. Though established in 1973, the synagogue had never had a rabbi. It began as just a handful of men gathering on Friday nights to pray together. "Those guys decided," recounts Kleinbaum, "'I don't want to have to choose between being deeply Jewish and openly gay.' That wasn't a revolution, but it *was*. Look what they created! It wasn't even a synagogue then. Up until 1973, if you were Jewish, you couldn't be gay. And if you were gay, you couldn't be Jewish." The number of

God on Our Side

 Frankly, a problem with the LGBT movement for liberation is that we've so often experienced religion as only a force for evil in the world: We haven't recognized the incredible power it can also be for liberation and change."

congregants grew exponentially, from ten to one hundred, to about 850 dues-paying synagogue members at present, and many others who regularly attend Friday night services or partake in many of the activities that CBST's staff of fifteen runs out of its loft office. The high holidays are another story altogether. New York's huge Jacob Javits Convention Center becomes home to thousands: Six thousand people came to pray at the Yom Kippur service after September 11, 2001.

But is was the AIDS crisis in part that prompted CBST's members to finally consider hiring their first rabbi. "AIDS took a terrible toll here," explains Rabbi Kleinbaum. "That is what I was hired for initially, to help shepherd the synagogue through this tremendous crisis. Probably 140 people here died from AIDS. When I came, it was really during the epicenter; we had deaths sometimes once a month, and several in the hospital at one time." In short, the congregation was decimated. Visitors to CBST will see a large memorial wall as they enter, with names of friends and family who died in the Holocaust on one side, and others who perished from AIDS on the other.

Leading the flock at CBST—or anywhere—was not at all in Sharon Kleinbaum's plans. "I never wanted to be a congregational rabbi. I thought congregations were bizarre." She had spent a few years at the National Yiddish Book Center, and then attended Philadelphia's Reconstructionist Rabbinical College, where they had just enacted a sexual nondiscrimination policy.

By now Kleinbaum had become very involved in political causes, AIDS work, and civil rights issues; wherever she felt wrong was being perpetrated. She was also becoming somewhat of a regular behind bars. Her participation in 1980's Women's Pentagon Action put her in prison for a month. In her usual style, Kleinbaum gives an extremely serious political moment a note of levity. "We thought we'd surround the Pentagon and shut it down. We used some cloth and we had some real hippies who were weaving the Pentagon shut. Affairs were happening in the gym—they kept us in a gym and we were sleeping with each other—lots of drama. I met a girl friend there who became a girlfriend for a few years; we met in jail." But this was hardly a humorous situation. "We were arrested for trespassing on federal property. I wasn't cooperating, so they wanted to punish us. There were nine of us. They took us away in shackles, nine little lesbians." It was there in federal prison that she was housed with the Manson women. "They were creepy," she says simply. (Rabbi Kleinbaum has hardly lost her radical touch. As recently as 2007, she was arrested with ACT UP's Larry Kramer and then–National Gay and Lesbian Task Force head Matt Foreman in an act of civil disobedience: a sit-in in the middle of Times Square.)

But suddenly, when presented with the opportunity at CBST, she realized that "creating community is a radical act." She says, "In a world in which people are so isolated, power is in community; I know that as an organizer and I know that as a religious person. You can't make people's lives better by snapping your finger, but you can be with people through really difficult things. People's lives can be transformed, and I felt like I could have a real impact."

At the forefront of her agenda is finding a way for sexuality and religion to intersect in the real world. "I think what has been changing is the recognition that religion has a significant role to play in the LGBT movement. There has been a recognition that if we both don't learn to respond to and be proactive about religion in America, we are losing a very significant battle. We're saying it's not just civil rights versus religious rights; we're saying, it's civil rights, yes, but its bigger than civil rights, it's human rights."

It doesn't sound like Rabbi Kleinbaum ever stops, not even for a second. She insists that she's "not a martyr," and that she and her longtime partner, Rabbi Margaret Moers Wenig, have had time to raise two daughters and actually take vacations, though when remains a mystery. Kleinbaum's quest to meld religion, human rights, and sexuality is not a job, or even a career, but a divine calling.

Over the course of a lifetime, one is bound to meet many clergy who are religious leaders. Rabbi Sharon Kleinbaum is a religious leader. But she would likely jump in here to add this: "A wonderful teacher of mine once said that I taught him that you don't have to be serious to be taken seriously. Because I believe in very big issues, but I really believe that you have to have a sense of humor about everything." This from someone who knows a little bit about joining together.

Sally Susman

"When I was a little girl growing up in St. Louis, I thought I really wanted to be the mayor of my town."

This is what little lesbian activists are made of: big, big dreams and, in this case, even bigger results. And Sally Susman has taken her activism to the next level: the boardrooms of corporate America. From American Express (twice) to Estée Lauder to Pfizer, where she is senior vice president and chief communications officer, Sally has pushed through two glass ceilings—not only as a woman in big business, but a gay one at that.

Sally's compass seemed to point east from very early in her life—evidently as soon as she began to set her sights higher than mayor. "St. Louis was not a tremendously easy place to grow up. It's a place where it's hard to be different. Whatever different *is*. I was eager to leave, eager to come to the East Coast." Though she was extremely competitive in school and in sports—she was a state champion tennis player—even then, Sally was already experiencing the *differentness*, though it was as yet unnamed. "I was always more interested in the girls than the boys. I don't think I really knew that word, *lesbian*, until I was in college and then began living as a lesbian right after college. But you know, crushes on best friends, camp counselor, the classic stuff."

But if Sally had an easy time coming out to herself, admitting it to her family was nowhere as simple. The upside is that it led her to LGBT activism when she first started her career in Washington, D.C. "My coming out to my parents was very difficult. We were enormously close before I came out, and we went through some very difficult years—now we are enormously close again. But during those difficult years, I felt like I needed a second home in a safe place, and I think in many ways that activist community fed me, and I felt appreciated, and I felt respected, and people wanted me to lead and be helpful."

Of course, her interest in activism didn't come out of the blue. Her father, Louis Susman, is presently ambassador to the Court of St. James. As Sally puts it, "I come from a family that wants to make change. My parents were always involved in politics and they worked hard for causes, and they continue to work hard for causes, and it's what I grew up with. It's what we talked about at the dining room table—in fact, my parents would require my brother and me to bring a news fact to the dinner table. And this was sort of the Socratic method over supper: 'What's the issue? How do you understand it? What do you think of it?'"

So it came as no surprise that Sally's first job was for the senator from Missouri (and former vice presidential candidate) Thomas Eagleton. The bloom was soon off the rose. "I saw that living all your life as a politician can be pretty brutal. So I wanted to work in government, because I wanted to make a difference, I wanted to make things better. It was very altruistic. But having spent six years on the Hill, I realized, you know, it's very frustrating to try to make change in government."

Two of those years were after Sally's first foray into corporate life, when she left Washington to work in New York at American Express. She returned to the capital to work as Deputy Assistant Secretary at the Department of Commerce. "I walked, I didn't run out of the closet" in Washington, she admits. "What happened was I came back to Washington to join the Clinton administration, and then there was to be a full background check for my position. And so, before I accepted the job, I told everybody I was gay."

Soon enough, however, Sally was back on the corporate track and happy to be there. "I came to believe that being well-positioned in powerful companies, you can be as much of a change agent, if not more so. And so being in the kind of role I'm in where my job is to bridge the public and the company—being part of company policymaking—has been a lot about the initial dream to be the mayor of my town."

In the meantime, Sally had found that she was what one friend called a "radical traditionalist" at heart. When she had come out to her parents years before,

her father had said, "You'll never have a career, a family, or children." Much has changed in the last quarter century, but Sally found there were indeed both cultural and legal hurdles ahead. It turned out her toughest experience being a lesbian didn't come from the boardroom, but the road to becoming a mother.

"Now it was the nineties, and I was really figuring out how I could become a mom. Because, this was a long time ago, and I think people may not appreciate that because, I mean, doesn't everybody have a baby now? We were the first of our friends, and I mean even our gay friends weren't sure it was such a good idea at the time." But Sally and her partner, Robin Canter, happily took the leap and brought daughter Lily home from China. Lily was only a few months old when Sally returned to work for a second time at American Express, this time stationed in London.

"Great, let's go live in Europe," we thought. "The

Coming Out on Capitol Hill

 It was very clear to me when I went to work for the Clinton administration that the biggest problem at that point was the 'secret,' not the fact. You know, a secret is more dangerous than a fact."

thing was—it's not the case now in England—they didn't recognize my partnership with Robin in the immigration status. So Robin had to quickly hustle, get her own job, get her own work permit, which is no small feat. But I can't tell you the bullets we were sweating. It was like, 'What are we going to do? And am I going to have to renege on this job? And a six-month-old baby? Can't do that.' It was a disaster, but we worked it out."

A few years later, Estée Lauder came calling, and Sally and her family were back in New York. "I've worked for three great companies. But," Sally notes with a laugh, "I really could say that I was a 'Lipstick Lesbian' when I worked for Lauder." Apparently she wasn't the only one who noticed. The lesbian character in the short-lived television drama *Cashmere Mafia* was, in fact, modeled after Sally. ("I was devastated when we were canceled!")

Now at Pfizer, in an era when health care is foremost in nearly every American's mind, Sally has an interesting take on her position. "Even though my title is chief communications officer, I see my role more broadly as being a listener for the company, helping the company to set a course on the public stage that's the right course for the company. Part of what makes my job really fascinating is finding the authoritative voices; getting those authoritative voices to speak on behalf of issues that we care about in health care."

Visiting Sally's office aerie, one is reminded of the

row house ever, consisting of just a long room upstairs, and one downstairs. It wasn't part of the original business plan: Greensgrow is buried in a warren of streets, surrounded on all sides by old factories and homes that have seen better days. But Corboy explained, "We needed a bathroom." It houses her office now, and at present an arugula-pesto-making franchise, which consists of a Cuisinart and a gray rubber bin, the kind usually carried around to bus dishes in a restaurant. This one's nearly full of the green gold, which will be spooned into plastic deli containers. Price: a mere $3.50. But then, Corboy is expert at making things work on the cheap. The house had no electricity and plumbing at the time, and it cost her $1,500.

But it's ingenuity that made Greensgrow one of America's premier urban farms; ingenuity and the mad desire of two recovering chefs to make absolutely fresh food available to restaurants, every day. It had nothing to do with a yen to try one's hand at farming. The thought never crossed Corboy's mind.

Mary Seton Corboy grew up in the midst of a big Irish family in Washington, D.C., and slogged through years of Catholic school, managing to squeak out of high school next to last in her class. Only after kicking around a few colleges and getting a master's degree in political science from Villanova did she discover an interest in learning—but in the meantime she had fallen in love with cooking.

Love did not conquer all, and she burned out fairly fast. "I had occasion to fire a couple of people, and they both came after me with knives. I figured it was time for a break—so I went to Wyoming, worked on a ranch, and cooked hot dogs for cowboys." After that came a stint as painter Andrew Wyeth's estate manager; so when she was ready for another change, she hardly expected a friend's attempt at growing heirloom tomatoes and lettuce in New Jersey to spark her interest.

"I was bored," she says now. "I went out to see what Tom was doing, and it was pretty pathetic." It wasn't long before she rolled up her sleeves and dove in. "I was living in Philadelphia," she muses, "and I hated going to New Jersey every day. I kept reading articles saying how there was so much abandoned land in the city. To me it was just a simple two plus two. We wanted to grow stuff, here was the land, and here was the market. We could grow everything hydroponically. Why were we going across the damn bridge every day?"

So move they did. In 1998, Mary and her partner, Tom Sereduk, bought a block in the Kensington section of the city for $25,000. They found half a dozen restaurant clients who felt the same way they did when they were chefs (desperate for really fresh ingredients) and they were on their way. The locals weren't particularly friendly. There was a lot of rock throwing and "faggot"-calling, but Mary insists it was mainly out of ignorance. (When Tom left the business a few years later, the neighbors felt bad, thinking his marriage had ended on the rocks.) Determined to rehab this asphalt jungle, Corboy went out on a frigid

Growing Through Food

 My vision as to what this place should be changed drastically over time. Now I see it as a community place—and now I mean community in the broadest sense: It should be something that makes the community a better place. Before I didn't know if this fence kept me on the inside or the outside of the zoo. . . . My willingness and ability to look at the community changed."

March day to begin the major cleanup, "only to realize the next day that this was the lot where everyone threw their beer cans on St. Patrick's Day."

"We didn't know anyone else who had a farm in the city," explains Corboy. "We just didn't know enough to know that it wasn't a good idea." When they went to agriculture schools like Penn State and asked them to come and give advice, they were consistently told that Greensgrow was breaking every rule. Even scarier was when they searched online for "urban agriculture," their farm was about the only thing that came up.

Even once they dug in, life was not exactly what they had pictured. "It seemed unstructured," Corboy recalls, "and of course it wasn't. You're governed by Mother Nature, by the seasons. We used to say, 'The first day it rains, we're going to go to some bar and eat chicken wings and drink beer.' It didn't rain the entire goddamn year. We couldn't get a day off to save our lives. And it didn't rain the next year. I think we went three years without any rain."

But the business started to . . . well, *grow*. The addition of a greenhouse allowed them to sell flowers—a high-cash, short-season portion of the farm's bottom line. Then Mary had an *aha* marketing moment one day while delivering food to a restaurant. She was talking about a CSA one of the chefs belonged to. (For the uninitiated, Community Supported Agriculture—often just called a food co-op—is an arrangement by which clients pay an annual fee upfront for a weekly portion of a farm's harvest. This provides the growers with seed money, in the realest sense of the phrase.) "'It's OK.' The chef shrugged. 'But I don't want all that zucchini and cabbage and stuff. My husband and I like gourmet salad greens and baby arugula. We like the stuff *you* grow.' I drove away and thought, 'We need a gay CSA. Little zucchinis, gourmet potatoes. Gear it toward the urban couple; folks learning to cook, who just bought their own first home and aren't going out as much.'" But the neighbors still didn't "get" Greensgrow. "They just thought we were bad growers. Everything we grew was so *tiny*."

Then, just as Greensgrow began to come into its own, Corboy found herself extremely ill with endometrial cancer ("Gay Girl Cancer," as she calls it). She was given four months to live. That was in 2004.

Mary Seton Corboy firmly believes that the country's farming and food buying habits are on the precipice of change, and that urban farming plays a huge part in its future. The extraordinary percentage that consumers habitually pay middlemen to get a vegetable from the farm to their table ranges from 64 to 75 percent, and the percentage of nutritional value and taste the food loses within forty-eight hours of being harvested is 40 to 60 percent. This needs to change. "I think there should be a place like Greensgrow in every city," Corboy insists. "It acts as a gathering place to meet and learn. It's an outdoor library of our times and of urban neighborhoods. It's a very interactive kind of place. Thinking, doing, moving, action all come into play at one time." And now the nonprofit arm of Greensgrow, the Philadelphia Project, adds farm lectures, school tours, workshops, and a barrage of ideas on how to grow the concept of urban agriculture into a nationwide reality.

"Lots of people who came to work here came because they believe in food and social justice as a part of urban agriculture. We constantly hunt for the middle ground so we can do what we need to do, and charge what's fair for everybody."

This from the woman who took up farming because she was bored. Now, when asked how she would define herself, Corboy quotes Collette: "You will do foolish things, but do them with enthusiasm."

It looks like Mary Seton Corboy can be counted on to continue doing foolish things and help to change the world . . . one tiny eggplant at a time.

Tenaja Jordon

Tenaja Jordan is a different kind of heroine. Just twenty-five years old, she is still pursuing her studies, working at her first important job, and finding her way. You won't see her on television, or as a platinum donor on an invitation. In her life thus far, her stock in trade has been bravery. And it's the bravery of ordinary people that makes the world go around and pushes history forward.

Tenaja is the kind of daughter any parents would be proud to have—*should* be proud to have. She grew up in Staten Island, New York, in an extremely close family. Yet as a young Jehovah's Witness, Tenaja felt her life—and how she was expected to live it—was planned for her from the start. "I had such a ridiculous religious upbringing: this is bad, that is bad; everything was about good and evil, right and wrong. There were no shades of gray, no, well, hmm, maybe this is all right. We didn't celebrate holidays or birthdays. Easter is bad; Christmas is bad; Thanksgiving is bad. There was no perspective. As a result, you begin to think about everything you do in those terms."

So when Tenaja started to realize very early that she liked girls, it gradually began to dawn on her that this would not go down easy in her world. "It wasn't until I was twelve or fourteen years old when I realized that some people would think this was wrong no matter how natural it feels to me," Jordan says, thinking back. "I had to make a choice then; I wasn't hurting anybody and nobody was hurting me—as long as I didn't say anything. I continued to hide my feelings because I just knew that I had to."

So far, Tenaja was on course, as far as her parents and teachers were concerned. She had won a citywide science prize, excelled in all her honors classes, and had been baptized into the family religion. But, like so many kids from time immemorial, "It was always about achieving, not for myself, but to try and please my parents." So when she started feeling dejected, confused, and began skipping school, Tenaja decided to take a risk, and in an attempt to take some control of her life, came out to her school guidance counselor. The very next day, she was called into the counselor's office.

"There were my parents, the assistant principal in charge of guidance, and the guidance counselor. I felt completely cornered. They suggested that recently I had seemed really stressed out, that I'd been holding something in, and telling me that if I had something to say that this was a safe space to say it in. I felt really pressured. If my parents hadn't known something was up, they certainly knew it now. I didn't feel safe at all; everything felt very hostile." Tenaja managed to

get through the meeting, and finally came out to her parents later that same day, at home.

"I got punished. I wasn't allowed to kiss or even hold my own brother and sisters because my parents thought that I was sick and diseased. They started treating me like I was a criminal because I was gay and because I had told them that I didn't believe in their religion; I thought that as long as I was doing this I might as well get it all out."

For most people, though it may still be a difficult process, coming out to one's parents is the beginning of a journey to personal freedom. Not so for Tenaja. She was forced to leave her religion, and her parents would never be allowed to speak to her again. So she sat down at her computer, searching for some help, and found the Hetrick-Martin Institute (HMI). It has long been a safe place in New York City for at-risk LGBTQ kids to find solace, services, and referrals. It is also home to the famed Harvey Milk High School. Tenaja will tell you that it saved her life.

"At the time, I was staying with a friend of mine up in the Bronx. I had no idea where I was going and on my last token. The HMI is on Astor Place and Broadway, so I was a long, long way from where I needed to be. Even though I was exhausted, once I finally got there, I realized that I'd come too far for this not to work.

"I didn't know what to think. I didn't know what to expect: I just had an address on one piece of paper and knew that I needed help. I arrived very early and I waited around for the other young kids to show up, and it was great; they were just like me. These guys look and sound like me."

But at seventeen, Tenaja was still underage. Over the next many months, she faced her mother in family court, lived in a children's center that was more like an institution, a homophobic foster home, and at last in an apartment that was part of an LGBT youth program.

Life finally began at eighteen. "Here I was living on my own," she recalls, "telling myself when to come and go. Remember, I didn't know much about anything: the Village, holidays, birthdays, nothing. So from eighteen until about twenty, I just learned about things. I would go to the pier, hang out in the Village, and just have fun."

But at twenty, Jordan was aging out of foster care, and needed a job beyond the one at the ice-cream store she currently had. And then another sort of miracle happened: SCO Family of Services, an agency dedicated for more than a hundred years to offering shelter and care to people in need—and the agency Tenaja was originally placed with—offered her a job. "It began with some surplus money left over from another program," Jordan explains. "They asked if, given the money, I could put together a series on internship programs for kids. So I did, for ninety-six kids. I was able to structure a program and give some kids work experience and help them qualify for housing when they are aging out."

Bringing It Home

"Every now and then I will tell a part of my story. I don't tell my entire story because kids can get mad and will use your story against you. Plus, I don't want my story to become the barometer. I think each child should set his own bar for success. Once in a while some kid will balk at going to therapy and I'll tell them that I go to therapy. Someone will tell me that they don't want to finish high school and I'll tell then that I almost didn't finish high school, but I applied myself."

If you believe that what goes around comes around, Tenaja's story is one that proves the adage. She never really left the Hetrick-Martine Institute, either; she is now a member of their board of directors. She is a social worker, helping kids just the way somebody helped her. Of course there's more to Tenaja Jordan's story, including more pain and some missteps—and there's plenty more to come. What makes her story extraordinary? It's the bravery of ordinary people. Heroism as the everyday. The hope, when you read how she survived and flourished, is that you have a little bit of Tenaja Jordan in yourself.

Of course, she says it best: "I think that I want to give back because of all the help that I've received along the way. I look at what some of these kids are going through and it is hell; they need help. It's pain, confusion, a sense of loss, and if you've ever felt that, you have an obligation to help somebody else who is going through the same thing."

Christine Vachon

"I am not into doing the right thing."

Now Christine Vachon doesn't mean that she's out looking to break the law. On the other hand, she's not against breaking the rules. In fact, that's what she's good at. It's what she's known for. Just to hear her say the above gives a Vachon fan a little thrill. Makes you wonder, "What is she up to now?"

Nearly two decades ago, the moniker "Godmother of New Queer Cinema" was coined for Christine Vachon. Just consider a few of the LGBT films she has shepherded: *Poison, Swoon, Go Fish, Stonewall, Party Monster, Far from Heaven*, and, of course, *Boys Don't Cry*—the movie that brought Hilary Swank a slew of awards, including an Academy Award for Best Actress in the role of a transgender young man named Brandon Teena. The world changed a little when *Boys Don't Cry* became a commercial success; not spin-off-its-axis changed, but enough to make a difference.

Vachon has, from the beginning of her career, been the kind of independent filmmaker you think of when you hear the phrase "a producer with a big vision, daring ideas, uncompromising ideals." And as the line between indie films and big-studio movies becomes blurred, Vachon and her team at Killer Films are still the real thing, putting films together bit by bit, dollar by dollar.

Killer is the home base of Vachon and partner Pamela Koffler and their staff, all working in a small bullpen of an office that is nearly as hushed as a library. No screaming moguls, not a limo or commissary in sight. In fact, the conversation at the moment is about recipes from the Silver Palate's Sheila Lukins, as phones jangle in the background. Out on the street, Christine turns a little more high-tech, juggling a couple of phones and deal points at once. Close up it doesn't seem like Hollywood, but if you eavesdrop, the action is all there.

Vachon has an aura of steadiness and gravitas about her; it's as if she's on an unwavering path to something—and she probably always has been. Born and raised in Manhattan to a mother who was French and a father who was a photographer for *Look* magazine, Christine's first foray into the arts began as a student at Music & Art High School, an experience she still cherishes. "I've never seen anything quite like it. It was the most diverse group of kids I'd ever seen. Because we were all united by a common interest—if not passion—for music or art, it broke down a lot of barriers. You'd spend one weekend at one kid's gigantic penthouse on the Upper East Side and then go hang out at another kid's house underneath the subway out on Long Island, and that was terrific."

Filmmaking wasn't taught in the seventies in public high schools in bankrupt New York City. "I think that it was far too expensive for anybody to do. They didn't have any film courses; there was no video at that time." But that all changed when she went off to Brown University (the only time Vachon has lived outside of New York City in her life) and their new, groundbreaking semiotics department.

"I didn't know what semiotics meant, nobody did. I think what happened is that I arrived at Brown and fell in with a group of people who were really challenging to me intellectually. I went to Paris my junior year and studied film theory there. Then I came back to Brown and they had a film program and a working filmmaker named Leandro Katz. By today's standards, kids would laugh at what that film program was: Everyone was sharing one 16mm camera and there was one editing facility. But we were all really into it and it was really fun."

When she returned to New York, Christine freelanced as a proofreader at a cable TV magazine. It was good money, and paid in cash. "It was almost as if we couldn't find enough things to spend it on! So we were having a great time, and friends started working on movies and we began production assisting and doing things like that. "

It was during this time that Vachon reconnoitered with Brown University acquaintance Todd Haynes. They have collaborated on many films, including *Velvet Goldmine*, *Far from Heaven*, and *I'm Not There*, but their first project together became a cult classic.

Acknowledgments

Everyone who heard about my burgeoning project helped me push it forward—until I realized that I was not at all alone in my belief that this was a book that, as my publisher Leslie Stoker said upon seeing the proposal, "was way overdue."

So many thanks to all the pros. My agent, Jennie Dunham, and all the wonderful folks at Abrams and Stewart, Tabori & Chang: the aforementioned Leslie Stoker, who got it from the get-go; my editor, Jennifer Levesque, who always knew right from wrong; Chalkley Calderwood, who quickly designed her way into my heart; my longtime friend, ally, and champion: sales and marketing guru Mary Wowk; Claire Bamundo, Kerry Liebling, Wesley Royce, and everyone else who helped me develop my dream of showcasing a group of very deserving women into a phenomenal piece of art. And of course, Abrams president and CEO Michael Jacobs, who took me out for a sandwich and gave me a book idea by dessert. Nice lunch.

Of course, it wouldn't have been a book at all without the wonderful Jennifer May—a great photographer and a game girl—and Chris Metze, her trusty better half: hard workers, great sports, and talented people, both. Plus, we had a ton of fun.

My heartfelt thanks to Steve Magnuson for his great advice, free hard work, much needed encouragement, and a movie when it was all too much; and to my legion of friends and family, who cheered me on and gave me great ideas.

To all the assistants, schedulers, publicists, and other aides too numerous to mention here, who paved the way to their bosses' calendars and hearts. You each understood how important this project was, and without your help and encouragement, the book would simply never have happened.

And of course, to all the women who agreed to grace the pages of *The L Life*: your stories pave the way for more freedom, more bravery, more people like you; I thank you from the bottom of my heart.